Working with sexually abused boys

AN INTRODUCTION
FOR PRACTITIONERS

D1824804

Jim Christopherson

Tillman Furniss

Brendan O'Mahoney

Anne Peake

with

Helen Armstrong & Anne Hollows

EDITED BY

Anne Hollows & Helen Armstrong

ISBN 0 902 81751 5
© NCB 1989

Cover illustration by Anne Bristow
Design, typesetting and artwork by Lasso Co-operative (01 272 9141)
Printed by Cathedral Press (0722 413122)

EDITORS' FOREWORD

In editing this collection of papers, we want to take this opportunity to highlight two concerns for the attention of readers.

The first relates to the 'state of the art' of work with boys and the fact that any publication in this newly emerging area of specialism is bound to be something of a hostage to fortune. These papers represent the views and researched information of a group of professionals from different backgrounds in the summer of 1989. Their very publication will create responses at both a practice and an intellectual level which will move along thinking and identify new areas for research – in fact will change the state of the art. So the impact of these papers upon the reader and their value as an immediate tool or a historical perspective will depend on how soon after publication you come to read them.

The second concern relates to perceptions about the prevalence and setting of abuse of boys. Acceptance is growing that the prevalence of sexual abuse among boys is higher than has been previously recognised. But there is a tendency to assume that boys are generally abused outside the family, perhaps because boys, more often than girls, are involved in sex rings. It is almost certain that boys are more often abused outside the family than are girls, but this should not limit the vigilance of professionals in any discipline to the possibility of intra familial abuse.

We are glad that the papers which follow are now being made available and are confident that they will contribute to better informed practice, training and research about the sexual abuse of boys. We look forward to receiving responses from a wide range of practitioners about their own work in this field and hope that further publications may enable a regular updating of knowledge and practice in this area of work.

ANNE HOLLOWS AND HELEN ARMSTRONG
National Children's Bureau
November 1989

Contents

■

Introduction

■

JIM CHRISTOPHERSON

This publication is the result of discussions by a working party set up under the auspices of the Training Advisory Group on the Sexual Abuse of Children to consider issues relating to the sexual abuse of boys. As the discussions developed, it became clear that the focus of the problem differed from the focus on work with girls where discussions of the sexual abuse of girls have tended to focus on incest and other forms of intrafamilial sexual abuse. With regard to boys, additional issues raised by the greater frequency of abuse outside the family must be considered. Some of the issues discussed by the working party, such as the problem of sex rings, of the handling of sexually abused youngsters in residential care or of the implications for black children who are sexually abused have relevance also to girls.

The working party was convened by Jim Christopherson, Lecturer in Social Work, University of Nottingham. Anne Peake, Psychologist, London Borough of Haringey, Dr. Tillman Furniss, Consultant Psychiatrist, Tavistock Clinic, and Brendon O'Mahoney, Project Manager, Barnardo's have written papers for the monograph. Anne Hollows and Helen Armstrong of the National Children's Bureau/TAGOSAC Training Project also attended the group and have written the concluding paper on training issues. Other people who attended the group were Rodney Smith, Principal, Glebe House, Prof. Donald West, Emeritus Professor of Criminology, University of Cambridge, Tom Woodhouse, then research student at the Institute of Criminology, Cambridge, George Douglas, Social Worker, Berkshire Social Services Department, and Terry Craven, Advice Worker, Walton Welfare Advice Centre, Liverpool. Widely different views emerged between the participants, and this publication should be seen in the context of the need to bring practice issues to public and professional attention rather than to lay down 'good practice' in the field in tablets of stone. Responsibility for the articles, therefore, is taken by those who wrote them.

Although English law forbids homosexual activity up to the age of twenty-one, we are concerned here with sexual abuse of boys under sixteen. We are dealing with paedophilia rather than homosexuality, and make no comment either way on whether or not homosexual involvement of teenagers over sixteen constitutes abuse.

Short articles have been collected which cover the similarities and differences between boys and girls in their experience of sexual abuse, on the implications for black children of sexual abuse, on the phenomenon of sex rings, on management issues in residential establishments, on planning and running group work, and on the particular needs of those who have been involved in sex rings. The publication is only an introduction to the topic, and we have not been able to cover intervention in great detail.

Under-reporting: the sexual abuse of boys

■

ANNE PEAKE

When one compares the numbers of cases of the sexual abuse of children that are reported either to the Police or the professionals, with the number of cases reported by the general population on confidential surveys, a pattern emerges. Firstly, that the majority of cases of child sexual abuse go unreported to the Police and professionals in the varying helping agencies. Secondly, that boys are even less likely to report sexual assaults than are girls. This paper looks at some of the reasons why there is considerable under-reporting about and by boy victims. More particularly, what is it about our society and our work as professionals, that has led to the present situation where boys are less likely than girls, to report their abuse.

Statistics of child sexual abuse

The numbers of cases of sexual assaults reported to the Police are low, see Table 1.

Sexual crimes amount to less than one per cent of the notifiable offences recorded in Police statistics. A small percentage figure, which appears at complete variance with impressions based on media reporting, particularly in the tabloid press. It is also notable that the overall number of offences is decreasing, unlike some other categories of crimes. For example over the same period (1974–1984) crimes of violence against the person increased considerably from 63,781 to 114,187 (West, 1987). The majority of the crimes are committed against females.

There are several reasons why such figures are likely to be an underestimate of the incidence of sexual crimes committed against children. Firstly, the way the law defines offences has a direct bearing on the statistics. For example, incest is defined by a specificity of the biological tie and the nature of the sexual contact; and so excludes

TABLE 1

Notifiable sexual offences recorded by the police
in 1974 and 1984 (Home Office, 1985)

Offence	1974	1984
Rape and attempts	1,052	1,433
Indecent assault on a female	12,417	10,837
Unlawful sexual intercourse with a girl under thirteen	304	270
Unlawful sexual intercourse with a girl under sixteen	4,746	2,622
Incest	337	290
Indecency with a child under fourteen	–	472
Buggery	587	602
Indecent assault on a male	3,096	2,321
Indecency between males	1,796	1,080
Procuration	67	102
Abduction	97	99
Bigamy	199	94
All sexual offences	24,698	20,222

instances, such as foster parent–child contact, abuse by professionals, and children being made to watch pornographic videos. These instances are defined as other offences, and they often then carry lower penalties. Secondly, the nature of offences committed against children are such that they usually take place in homes where there are no witnesses other than the abuser and the child or other children. So issues of corroboration, the admissability of evidence, and the ethics of cross-examining children in court, contribute to the difficulties of proving the offences. Without proof the offences do not figure in Police statistics. Thirdly, once it has been established by the Police that there may be a basis for a charge, the advice of the Director of Public Prosecutions (DPP) must be sought. A decision to prosecute will then be made if it is believed to have a reasonable prospect of securing a conviction. As noted issues of proof in instances of sexual crimes committed against children are complex and difficult to establish. Fourthly, children, families, and professionals, are often reluctant to report offences as they fear the consequences of disclosure. When cases are reported there are often huge delays prior to cases coming to court. When cases reach the courts, in the absence of guilty pleas, it can be harrowing for the child to give evidence and face cross-examination. Support for the child and family after a prosecution is often piecemeal or non-existent. So the process of the law is seen as punitive rather than reforming. In summary, definitions of offences, the nature of the offences, the problems of securing convictions, and the fears of children, parents, and professionals, combine to lead to low levels of reporting sexual abuse to the Police.

From a basis of current Police statistics it is not possible to estimate whether there are different levels of reporting in girl and boy victims. Reported crimes against boys are much lower than crimes against girls. What proportion they are of the real incidence of such crimes would be debatable. However, a comparison of statistics collected by professionals and in confidential surveys sheds some light.

Substantially more cases of child sexual abuse are reported to professionals. The most recent review of the incidence of child sexual abuse in the United Kingdom looked at the numbers of cases of abuse both within and outside the family, reported to professionals (Mrazel, Lynch and Bentovim, 1981). The study looked at the extent to which professionals recognised or were referred cases of child sexual abuse. Sexual abuse was defined as: Type I, battered child whose injuries are primarily in the genital area. Type II, child who has experienced attempted or actual intercourse or other inappropriate genital contact with an adult. Type III, child who has been inappropriately involved with an adult in sexual activities, not covered by I and II. The survey revealed that in the majority of the cases of child sexual abuse reported to professionals, 73.5% of cases, the abuser was known to the child beforehand. The authors estimated that the incidence rate was 1,500–1,600 new cases per year. Projecting these figures for the child population as a whole, they suggest a minimum number of three per 1,000 children could be recognised by a professional as having been sexually abused at some point in their childhood. This gives a figure of .3% of the population.

The survey looked at both the frequency that abused children were seen over a target year and in some detail at the most recent cases seen. The figures looking at frequency are remarkably incomplete with regard to the gender of the children. The study quotes girls 42%, boys 7%, and gender not specified 51%. This certainly suggests that the authors of the study were not considering how the impact of the problem might be different for boys and girls (demonstrated in the way the study questionnaires were framed and/or the professionals circulated). In the survey of the most recent cases seen, there is a suggested ratio of 84:16, girls to boys, see Table 2.

So professionals see mainly female victims of abuse. How far this figure reflects the expectations of professionals, or the levels of reporting by boys and girls, or the actual incidence of abuse remains unanswered. Results produced by confidential surveys suggest that not only are the

TABLE 2

Age and sex of last case seen by professionals
(Mrazek, Lynch and Bentovim, 1981)

Age	Girls	Boys
0 – 5 years	12%	–
6 – 10 years	19%	6%
11 – 15 years	50%	7%
Not given	3%	3%

numbers of children offended against greater than in Police and professional figures, but also that the ratio of girls to boys is different.

A recent British survey revealed that 12% of women and 8% of men report childhood experiences of sexual abuse (Baker and Duncan, 1985). The survey was conducted by female interviewers using confidential one to one interviews conducted in the respondents' homes. The abuse reported ranged from being talked to in an erotic way, exhibitionism, to being handled/masturbated, to full sexual intercourse. The survey collected information according to gender, see Table 3.

What the survey revealed was a greater incidence of the problem of child sexual abuse, 10% of the general population. Although the numbers are much higher, the method of the survey was such that false positives

TABLE 3

Patterns of sexual abuse (Baker and Duncan, 1985)

	Male %	Female %
Intrafamilial	13	14
Extrafamilial	44	30
Stranger	43	56
One-off incident	59	66
Repeated (same person)	30	18
Multiple abusers	11	16
No contact	48	55
Contact	49	40
Intercourse	5	5

were unlikely, and if anything, the estimate of incidence is likely to be an underestimate. The survey indicates a ratio of 60:40, girls to boys, a considerably different ratio from that reported by professionals.

Why children can't tell

A comparison of the statistics of child sexual abuse collated by Police, professionals and in a confidential survey, suggests that there is under-reporting by victims, particularly male victims. If we are to create a climate in society and in our professional work where children are able to tell, then we need to consider how under-reporting reflects society's and professionals' capacities to hear and protect children. Children can't tell about sexual abuse for many reasons. Three general reasons stem from the nature of child sexual abuse: (Peake, 1988a).

First, children do not have the language and/or the permission to tell about what is happening to them. Many of the children are too young to use language or to have the words to describe what is happening and how they feel. Children in our society are taught to obey known adults/parents. If a child can't trust a parent or familiar adult then to whom can a child go to be believed? The children tell us 'no-one'. Children often do not have permission to tell about approaches by familiar adults, though child sexual assault prevention programmes are beginning to tackle this problem (Elliott, 1985). Sadly, some children do tell, often in tentative or oblique ways; only to find what they say is ignored, discounted, or disbelieved.

Second, many children are subject to actual or implied threats not to tell. Children who witness violence in the home committed against adults and/or children need not even be threatened to know what would be the probable consequences of telling. When children are subjected to threats they are unaware how they may be protected from the threats being carried out. Often a child will be made aware that his or her silence about the abuse maintains a precarious balance in which appearances are maintained, and the non-abusing parent and/or siblings are protected, or so children believe. From a very young age children learn from situational cues that what is happening is not to be talked about. As they grow older, they learn that what is happening is wrong. While 'Childline' tries to help children tell, the Cleveland Inquiry has shown them that child sexual abuse provokes massive adult disagreement, and disbelief. Children have no basis on which to evaluate their situation. The alternatives to being abused are unknown, and they can only fear they will exchange one kind of unhappiness for another.

Third, children may be unable to recognise the abusive experience as abuse, having been tricked or bribed into acquiescence. Children by virtue of their innocence can be tricked into not telling, believing the abuse to be part of an affectionate parenting role. The abusive experience may be all the child receives in response to his/her need to be wanted and held, and so the child may love and be reluctant to betray the abuser. The child may well have the position of a 'favoured' child emotionally and/or materially, and have been rewarded for his/her acquiescence. Children can be overwhelmed by their own responses and see them as indicative of their guilt and responsibility for the abuse, and so not tell.

The pressures on children not to tell about sexual abuse are many. The difference between the numbers who are recognised by or referred to professionals, .3% (Mrazek, Lynch and Bentovim, 1981), and those who report their own experiences in a confidential survey, 10% (Baker and Duncan, 1985), show quite clearly that many do not tell. In considering what we know about the sexual abuse of boys in particular, it is important to always bear in mind that those whose abuse is reported to the Police, and/or recognised by or referred to professionals, are only a proportion of victims. There is no basis for assuming that the victims of child sexual abuse are a homogeneous group. Such assumptions have been made in the past; for example the seductive child notion (discussed in Meiselman, 1978), the idea that abuse is an accepted part of some subcultures (Lucianowicz, 1972), and the notion of a cycle of abuse – victim/failed parent or abuser. Such conclusions were drawn without any realisation of how many children's lives are affected by sexual assaults. Ironically such notions, while part of attempts to understand the problem, may well have contributed to the fact that children can't tell what is happening.

The sexual abuse of boys

What we know of the sexual abuse of boys is limited. For the purposes of this paper, I have focussed on what is revealed by the UK study (Baker and Duncan, 1985); as other attempts to look at the incidence and nature of sexual abuse are limited by either looking only at female populations (Russell, 1983), or selected populations (college students -- Finkelhor, 1979), patients of a psychiatric clinic – (Meiselman, 1978), or at characteristics of reported cases of abuse (Finkelhor, 1984).

The Baker and Duncan (1985) study indicates that 8% of men report such instances from their childhood years. The suggestion is that the average age at which boys are assaulted is 12.03 years. It seems that boys are more at risk during the early teenage years and are at risk from acquaintances outside the family and in positions of trust. Boys are less at risk from strangers. Boys are also more likely to be subjected to ongoing abuse but less likely to be the victims of more than one abuser. More men report their abuse as having included instances of sexual contact. Both men and women seem to have been equally subjected to intercourse.

Results of the survey echo many previous studies (Renvoize, 1982, Herman, 1981) in reporting that the experience does not determine the outcome, short or long term. Many survivors see their experiences as having an adverse effect on their lives which endures, and for many does not diminish. Sexual abuse cannot be measured by the nature of the sexual act. The essence of the abuse is an abuse of power, implicit in the imbalance of age, size, understanding, and power, between an adult and a child; and a betrayal of trust, an accepted basic component of familiarity between adults and children. Children are less likely to be damaged if the assault is not repeated, if the abuser is a stranger, and if the child is believed and supported following disclosure.

One notable gender difference in the responses to the survey was in the attitudes of men and women to their experiences of abuse, see Table 4.

TABLE 4

Subjective reports of abuse (Baker and Duncan, 1985)

	Male	Female
Harmful at the time	33%	57%
Permanent damage	4%	13%
No effect	57%	34%
Improved life	6%	2%

Attitudes to the abuse also varied with the age abuse began, the frequency of the abuse, the identity of the abuser, and the age of the respondant at interview. Given the focus of the present discussion, it is useful to consider the effect of gender on attitudes to abusive experiences. It does seem that the meanings attached to gender in our society may well underpin why boys are less likely to be recognised as abused, and to report their abuse.

Issues of under-reporting
'Boys get molested too', said Tony, 'so how come all these leaflets are about girls? ... and if as you say, it happens to lots of boys, how come there's only four of us in this group?' These were disarming questions in the course of a group run to help boys who had been sexually abused by adults known to them. Professionals and the general public need to

consider what it is about our society which has led to the present situation where boys are less likely than girls to report their abuse. The following issues are suggested as underpinning the under-reporting of the sexual abuse of boys.

The male ethic of self reliance

There continue to be differences in the way the two genders are socialised (St. John-Brooks, 1982). The toys and clothes of childhood, together with the language adults use about children, baby boys are usually admired for being big, strong and active, girls for being slim, pretty and gentle; tell us that we continue to set very different expectations for girls and boys. Particularly with regard to being hurt and self reliance, adult expectations of children, in terms of the gender of the child, are very different. When children hit each other, we expect or are not surprised, when a girl cries, but we tell a boy to 'hit back'. Society's definition of masculinity does not expect males to express feelings of dependency, fear, vulnerability or helplessness (Nasjleti, 1980). Most boys are expected to be able to defend themselves from the aggression of others.

These differences can lead to differences in the reporting of sexual abuse by girls and boys. The general public just simply does not expect boys to be victims. For example, self defence classes are usually for girls/women, the 'Childline' poster features a young girl, until this year there was no rape crisis organisation or counselling for men, and when men do talk about their victimisation (for example in television documentaries such as 'Crime of Violence' Channel 4) their anonymity is preserved. The overwhelming message is that boys/men should be able to rebuff or handle assaults, and that if they don't, there is something about talking about what happened that would affect the regard with which they are held in the future. It is small wonder that male victims report that they feel they should have been in control of the situation and are ashamed to have been a victim (Monaco and Gaier, 1988). Our society does not encourage boys/men to complain when they are hurt, rather the ethos is one of keeping quiet or of retaliation.

Notions of youthful male sexuality

There is a sense in our society, that early sexual experiences are somehow a part of most boys' lives. As adults and parents we continue to prefer girls to be innocent, and expect boys to be worldly wise. The effects of this are seen most sharply in the ratio of girls to boys admitted to care as being 'beyond parental control', over 2 girls to every boy (Peake, 1979). It can also be seen in the language we use. For example, there are a number of words in common parlance to describe girls who have had early sexual experiences. Many of these have quite derogatory connotations, 'bike', 'slag', 'whore', 'slut', etc. The number of words compares quite sharply with the fact that there are far fewer words to describe boys who are similarly experienced, and for some, the words are not considered derogatory at all; for example compare the word 'whore' with the word 'stud'.

The idea that early sexual experiences are a part of a boy's adolescence leaves many boys who are assaulted feeling quite unclear about whether the experience is a 'rite of passage' or an assault. Boys are more likely than girls to be assaulted together with others, either with siblings or with other boys. As Finkelhor (1984) points out, one of the main ways in which boys are identified is when a sister discloses or the abuse of a sister is discovered. The fact that boys are more often abused in groups means they are less likely to report, as they are confused about whether the experience is an assault or just what happens to boys (Monaco and Gaier, 1988). The presence of other boys can often seem to confirm the latter and also serve to inhibit telling, no one boy wanting to be the first to tell.

More freedom to lose

Families tend to supervise and restrict the freedom of girls more than of boys. The reminders that girls and women are vulnerable to assault are contained in society's view that females are sex objects; for example, partially clad women feature regularly in some daily papers, women's bodies are used in advertising, even to sell car tyres, sexual harassment and violence are a part of today's news. What thinking parent/adult would not be aware of the threats to girls and the need to be vigilant in their defence?

The under-reporting of assaults on boys together with the ethic of self reliance for boys has led to the fact that parents are more apt to warn their daughters of the dangers of assault (Monaco and Gaier, 1988). The absence of specific teaching about the nature of sexual assault and strategies for being able to seek help and to tell, being directed specifically at boys, leaves them vulnerable and unsure what they should do if they are victims. Given boys are allowed more freedom, the subsequent anxiety and increased level of supervision by adults that so often follows the discovery/disclosure of child sexual abuse, can lead some boys to be reluctant to talk about what has happened to them. They fear if they tell, they won't be allowed to go out again by themselves.

The stigma of abuse and the implications for the boys' sexuality

Many victims question themselves when they are assaulted. Their sense of self doubt, embarrassment, and shame, leads many to feel, quite wrongly, that they themselves provoked the attack. An abuser may well have implied as much as a way of securing the child's compliance and silence.

As is the case for girls, the majority of boys are assaulted by men, 96% (Reinhart, 1987). Boys frequently express shame at not being dominant (Nasjleti, 1980). They see their abuse as an indication that they are homosexual. This can lead to under-reporting, particularly when boys are aware of society's intolerence towards homosexuals; for example as shown in the frequent references in the tabloid press to aids as 'a gay plague', and in the polarising views on the question of promoting positive images of homosexuality. Boys can question their passivity as victims and their own masculinity. Much of their socialisation has ill prepared them for the feelings of being a victim. Even the nature of their abuse, by the same sex adult, confirms a view of men as controlling and dominant. For some boys and men, the only way they can overcome the feelings of a victim is by exerting their power, either through revenge on the abuser or by attacks on others (Kreps, 1987). Work with adolescent sex offenders has revealed a high percentage were themselves victims of a sexual assault. Often the offences are dismissed as 'boys will be boys' or labelled as curiosity and experimentation (Ryan et al, 1987). Attempts to dismiss or punish the behaviour of juvenile sex offenders obscure the extent to which such behaviour is a learned response to assert one's masculinity following abusive experiences.

Ironically, notions of a cycle of abuse, particularly with regard to boys, the cycle of victim become abuser, may well deter many adult men from telling about childhood abuse. Few men would be willing to speak while professionals remain so general and unclear in their views about this cycle of abuse. As mentioned earlier, there is no evidence that the victims of abuse are a homogeneous group. Men who speak out today risk the labelling that women have faced and known for years.

The effect of perceived agency roles
When considering why boys don't report sexual abuse, it is important to consider their perceptions of the agencies to whom we expect them to report. These are Social Services/NSPCC, the related helping professions such as Child Guidance, and the Police.

Social Services/NSPCC are primarily concerned with intrafamilial abuse, as these agencies are charged with a child protection role. The warning signs cf abuse; especially in teenage girls, such as eating problems, running away, suicide attempts, are more likely to alert the child guidance, child protection services. The workers are aware of the problem of sexual abuse for girls and so more girls are recognised. Often the services aim to facilitate disclosures, and to offer help in terms of counselling, family therapy, and groupwork. So girls who consider telling tend to approach these agencies.

In contrast, boys are more likely to display acting out behaviours as warning signs of abuse; such as aggression, delinquency and sexual offending. These behaviours are seen as potentially threatening and so are often dealt with at face value and in a punitive way, by either Social Services and/or the Police. There is often a failure to recognise the difficult behaviour of some boys as a consequence of and reaction to abuse. As Finkelhor (1984) points out the model of the dysfunctional family in which fathers become sexually involved with their daughters when their marital relationship has broken down, if it applies at all, can apply only to the abuse of girls. There has been a lack of awareness of the extent to which boys are also subjected to sexual abuse and this has led to professional disbelief (Nasjleti, 1980).

In addition, boys are more likely to be assaulted by adults known to them but outside the family (see Table 3). Extrafamilial abuse presents fewer dilemmas for the family and professionals and so is more likely to be viewed as a crime, and reported to the Police. Without evidence or a guilty plea there is often little the Police can do. The Police also do not offer treatment resources. The extent to which boys view the Police positively as an agency to which one can go when hurt, will have a direct bearing on the likelihood of boys telling. The guilt and self doubt so often felt by victims, for boys may well militate against telling the Police, who have additional roles; for example, apprehending the guilty, checking the reliability of statements, etc.

The power of the paedophile lobby

It is more comfortable for the general public, parents, and professionals, to believe that adults who sexually assault children are isolated, odd individuals. Unfortunately this is far from the truth. A substantial proportion, 49% according to Baker and Duncan (1985), are known to the children beforehand, and so are in positions of familiarity and trust for the children. The remainder are said to be 'strangers'. It is not possible to calculate how many of all abusers are paedophiles. However, recent cases, such as the Leeds sex ring concern, reveal that a proportion of all abusers choose their families, their jobs, and their friends, with a view to gaining access to children. Evidence as to the extent of the problem is limited in so far as much of the information on paedophilia comes from known convicted adults, and the general public prefers to consider the problem to be a minor one, and so underestimates the problem. Paedophiles are almost always men and in the main indicate a preference for boys (Righton, 1981).

Far from being isolated odd individuals, they are often qualified, well connected men with some social standing. For example, the most recent convictions of men involved in the Paedophile Information Exchange were two men – one has a Ph.D. degree and the other was a mathematics teacher, a Principal Educational Psychologist was gaoled for sexually assaulting children, a Paediatrician from St. George's Hospital was convicted of collecting indecent photographs of children, senior staff of the UNICEF organisation in several countries have been arrested on suspicion of sexual offences against children.

An unknown proportion of those promoting adult-child sexual contacts are intelligent, with positions of responsibility, and often they are part of considerable networks of like-minded people. Faced with this, the under-reporting of boys is understandable, and inevitable. If boys are to feel they can tell, then child protection agencies need to help the general public and parents to separate arguments about the age of consent and penal reform from discussions of child sexual abuse, and to recognise and tackle the problem of child pornography. While judges continue to describe collecting pornographic pictures of children as 'puerile like collecting cigarette cards', we will continue to under-estimate the problem and make it impossible for some boys to tell.

The way forward
What does become clear from a consideration of the under-reporting of the sexual abuse of boys, is that the issues are complex. Information and insight into the sexual abuse of girls was primarily promoted by the women's movement, when adult survivors of violence in the home, rape and child sexual abuse, began to speak out, make links with each other, and form self help groups. The courage of these women helped children by articulating their fears, providing help, and a model of survival. Perhaps what we need now are adult male survivors to take those same risks for the sake of the boys and to challenge and inform what we know of the sexual abuse of boys.

There remains a great deal that professionals can contribute to facilitate the recognition/disclosure of sexual abuse of boys. The following suggestions came out of this discussion of the issues of under-reporting:

1. **Collect gender based statistics.** Feminists have for a long time had gender issues as a main feature of their approach to child sexual abuse. Professionals involved in research and clinical practice need to prioritise gender issues as a way of collecting clearer information and of communicating a willingness to recognise and respond to the sexual abuse of boys.

2. **Re-evaluate the theories of sexual abuse.** The ratio of women to men reporting childhood experiences of sexual abuse in a confidential survey reveals larger numbers of men who have been victims of abuse than had previously been known to the police and professionals. The numbers of boys involved; together with other factors not discussed in detail in this paper, such as the high levels of recidivism among abusers, challenge theories about the dysfunctional family and the notion of the cycle of abuse, boy victim-adult offender. The theories need continued debate and challenge.

3. **Debate the implications of the gender of the worker.** The vast majority of abusers are men. It has been suggested that this fact springs from the features of the differences with which children are socialised according to gender. Male socialisation with its features of: fear of intimacy, the premium placed on force, the undervaluing of women and 'feminine' attributes, and the splitting off of the sexual act from emotional and relationship contexts, underpins the preponderance of male abusers (Frosh, 1988) and has consequences for the children. For abused children, relationships with men are at the core of their pain. Yet nothing raises controversy like the suggestion that we debate the impact of male workers on help given to abused children. The arguments are many: the contribution of a 'real' professional is more than his/her gender, children should have female key workers to give them a sense of safety, abused children need positive male models, abused children need to work through their trauma with men, and so on. Rarely is the debate a calm one, for it challenges assumptions of our professional hierarchies, and rarely are child centred decisions made. The decisions are usually about what we've always done, the irrelevance of gender, and the impracticalities of staff allocation according to gender. We need to debate this.

4. **Develop an awareness of gender differences in the indicators and effects of sexual abuse.** Differences in reporting may well be due in part to professionals, parents, and the general public, not being aware of the indicators of abuse for boys (Sebold, 1987). For example, exhibitionism and sexual offending in pre-adolescent/ adolescent boys is often not seen as an indication that the boys may have been abused, and the boys are punished rather than helped to talk about what has prompted them to behave thus. Work on the indicators and effects of abuse in boys would help professionals to recognise boys at risk.

5. **Public/professional debate about the adverse effects of sexual abuse for both girls and boys.** While there continue to be differences in the ways we socialise our children according to gender, there will be confusion about the distinction between youthful male sexuality and abuse. The confusion will limit the numbers of boys reporting and hinder the debate about the harmful effects of abuse, by depicting the experiences of the boys as less victimising than they are (Finkelhor, 1984).

6. **Use prevention programmes to highlight the risk to boys and girls.** Prevention programmes need to make clear the risks to boys as well as girls. If attention is paid to gender then the materials in the programmes can be used to prepare boys for such approaches, and to signal that this does happen to boys and so facilitate telling. Along the same lines, there could be a 'Childline' poster showing a boy.

7. **Use prevention programmes to address the barriers to reporting.** Children by their innocence and dependence are unable to see the essence of their abuse, the misuse of power and the betrayal of trust. Prevention programmes need to avoid presenting an over simple view of the risks to children of sexual assault. It is all too easy to reduce the concepts in programmes of direct work with children to learning about 'yes' and 'no' feelings, to say no, and to tell of approaches by adults (Peake, 1988b). Programmes need to deal with uncertainty about what is abuse, self blame in children, and the reasons why children can't tell. (Monaco and Gaier, 1988). Helping children understand the barriers to telling can be one way of relieving them of the additional guilt of silence.

8. **Research into child pornography.** There continues to be a great deal of confusion about the nature of the offence and offenders of child sexual abuse. Most people feel child pornography is wrong, but most are unclear what part pornography plays in any sexual assault on a child. We prefer to believe that child pornography is a limited concern; that it has no connections with the everyday techniques of the media, dressing small children as adults to sell products and using undressed young women to sell newspapers. So long as we prefer to believe child pornography is not the widespread organised financial business that it is, we ignore the reality of risks to children and stifle the debate. While we continue to believe men who assault children are isolated odd individuals, rather than a product of the society in which we live, we preserve our naivety at the expense of children. So much pornography features children and women because they are the less valued, less powerful members of our society.

9. **More men to speak out.** There is a need for more adult male survivors to take the risks involved in speaking about their abuse. Without them, boys who are currently being abused do believe themselves to be the only person to whom this has happened and the boys are denied the positive models for telling and for surviving. If more men, speak out, then the notion of the cycle of victim/abuser can be challenged. Perhaps what the rest of us can do, is to consider seriously what we do and think that makes the risks, faced by survivors speaking about their experiences of being assaulted. Do we really not blame the victims, or do we actually think that victims make poor parents and over-involved professionals? Perhaps what we do and think makes it inevitable that male survivors will opt for anonymity. When the 'rule book' says you should be in control, there's too much to lose by admitting you were not and how hurt and upset you are.

10. **A continued striving for equal opportunities.** The factors which underpin why children and women are so vulnerable to violence and sexual assault are pervasive throughout our society. Our society remains one in which men and women are not treated equally and with fairness. The majority of assaults are committed by men. Children will continue to find it difficult to tell while the majority of positions of power and responsibility are held by men and while there remains a sense in which we do not value children in their own right, for example poor maternity pay and leave, the abolition of the maternity grant, limited creche and nursery facilities, few workplace allowances made for women's dual role (McConville 1987). If the power and opportunities of our society were shared more equally, there could then be the sense in which men need not be self reliant and in control, and women could have the support and resources to separate from abusers.

Bibliography

Baker A. and Duncan S. (1985) 'Child Sexual Abuse: A Study of Prevalence in Great Britain'. Journal of Child Abuse and Neglect, Vol.9, pp.457–467.
Elliott M. (1985) 'Preventing Child Sexual Assault'. Bedford Square Press.
Finkelhor D. (1979) 'Sexually Victimised Children'. The Free Press.
Finkelhor D. (1984) 'Child Sexual Abuse: New Theory and Research'. Free Press.
Finkelhor D. and Horaling G.T. (1984) 'Sexual Abuse in the National Incidence Study of Child Abuse and Neglect: An Approach'. Journal of Child Abuse and Neglect, Vol.8 pp.23–33.
Frosh S. (1988) 'No Man's Land?: The Role of Men Working with Sexually Abused Children'. British Journal of Guidance and Counselling, Vol.16 No.1.

Herman J.L. (1981) 'Father-Daughter Incest'. Harvard University Press.

Home Office (1985) 'Criminal Statistics – England and Wales, 1984'. HMSO.

Kreps A. (1987) 'Breaking the Silence on a Taboo Subject'. The Listener, 23 July 1987.

Lucianowicz N. (1972) 'Incest: Paternal Incest II, Other Types of Incest'. British Journal of Psychiatry, p.120.

McConville B. (1987) 'Mad to be a Mother'. Century.

Meiselman K.C. (1978) 'Incest: A Psychological Study of Causes and Effects with Treatment Recogmmendations'. Jossey Bass.

Monaco N.M. and Gaier E.L. (1988) 'Differential Patterns of Disclosure of Child Abuse Among Boys and Girls: Implications for Practitioners'. Early Child Development and Care. Vol.30 pp.97–103.

Mrazel P.B., Lynch M., and Bentovim A. (1981) 'Recognition of Child Sexual Abuse in the United Kingdom', in 'Sexually Abused Children and Their Families'. (Edit) Mrazel P.B. and Kempe C.H. (1981). Pergamon Press.

Nasjleti M. (1980) 'Suffering in Silence: The Male Incest Victim'. Child Welfare, Vol.LIX, No.5.

Peake C.A.E. (1979) 'A Comparison of the Characteristics of Boys and Girls Admitted to Observation and Assessment Centres'. Unpublished M.Sc. Thesis, Manchester University.

Peake A. (1988a) 'Why Children Can't Tell About Sexual Abuse'. Church of England Children's Society.

Peake A. (1988b) 'A Discussion Paper re. Child Sexual Assault Prevention Programmes in Schools'. Church of England Children's Society.

Reinhart M.A. (1987) 'Sexually Abused Boys'. Journal of Child Abuse and Neglect, Vol.II, pp.229–235.

Renvoize J. (1982) 'Incest: A Family Pattern'. Routledge and Kegan Paul.

Righton P. (1981) 'The Adult' in 'Perspectives on Paedophilia'. Taylor B. (Edit). Batsford Academic.

Russell D.E.H. (1983) 'The Incidence and Prevalence of Intrafamilial Sexual Abuse of Female Children'. Journal of Child Abuse and Neglect, Vol.3, pp.953–957.

Ryan G., Lane S., Davis J. and Isaac C. (1987) 'Juvenile Sex Offenders: Development and Correction'. Journal of Child Abuse and Neglect, Vol.II, p.385–395.

Sebold J. (1987) 'Indicators of Child Sexual Abuse in Males'. Social Casework: The Journal of Contemporary Social Work, February 1987.

St. John-Brooks C. (1982) 'Must girls always be girls?' New Society, 1 April 1982, p.10.

West D.J. (1987) 'Sexual Crimes and Confrontations'. Gower.

Sexually abused boys and girls: comparisons and contrasts

∎

BRENDAN O'MAHONEY

Victims

The victims of sexual abuse can range from infants and toddlers to children and teenagers. They are both male and female. They are helpless young people who can be easily exploited, bribed or coerced. The common consensus is that sexual acts between an adult and a young person are, of their nature, harmful. This is because such acts are engaged in for the benefit of the adult and not that of the individual boy or girl.

James and Nasjleti[1] argue that a relationship between a young person and an adult that causes severe emotional distress is harmful to that young person's development. Such distress would be caused by a loss of childhood innocence; an alienation from peers; an inability of the young person to cope with powerful adults in a lover role; a pressure on the child who is singled out from siblings and peers as special; the burden of keeping a relationship secret from others; the experience of emotions too powerful to be worked through with a child's mental mechanism; an overloading stimulation and insufficient tension relief; and, in the case of incest, the forming of an alliance with one parent against another.

Victimisers

Traditionally sexual abuse has been seen as a crime where the victim is female and the victimiser male. It is clear, however, that both boys and girls are victims of an abuse of power by adults who use their youth, their weakness, their lack of knowledge and their dependence on adults to take advantage of them. Young people are subject to threats of physical harm to themselves or to members of their families and are blackmailed by a withdrawal of affection, love and attention if a parent is involved.

Both boys and girls are likely to be abused by older males. For girls it is likely that the abuser is the father or a father-type figure such as a stepfather or a man living with the mother. A study by Robert and Lois Pierce in 1985[2] found that for boys the victimiser was more likely to be a stepfather and for girls the natural father. They felt that this was an expected statistic given the fact that in their sample males were less likely to reside with their natural fathers. Boys, however, were also less likely to be abused by their natural fathers when the perpetrator was a father figure.

Both boys and girls can be abused by siblings and this is likely to occur in those families where an adult is sexually abusive and where role boundaries are confused or non-existent. In such families parents do not meet their children's needs for love, affection and nurturance.

Young people are also molested by men who are unrelated and unknown to them. These are likely to be adults whose psycho-social development has been severely damaged by their own experiences of abuse and their inability to maintain intimate relationships with other adults.

There are also younger men, sometimes adolescents, who are frightened of relationships with peers and find safety and a sense of control when relating to young children, male or female. For these people the child is the stimulator. By relating to a child sexually they feel they are in control and have mastered situations where, often as not, they have had no control as young children and where they themselves were very likely victims.

The least reported incidents are those where the abuser is a woman; often the mother or a mother-figure. The victims of this form of abuse can exhibit more confusion than other victims. They have feelings of both love and hate towards the woman/mother, feelings of self-loathing, and feelings of responsibility for what has taken place. In their eyes they have betrayed a parent by telling and will make great efforts to describe the mother's behaviour as acceptable, underlying their belief in her as a good parent. Boy victims may often be in a role reversal situation in a family which has an absent father, yet at the same time they are expected to behave as young children. Girl victims often behave as extensions of the mothers with the same extreme dependency needs. Boy victims have difficulty in reporting this form of abuse lest their sexuality may be called into question. They also fear that it may expose some real or imaginary sexual abnormality in their lives.

Responses to abuse

There are differing definitions as to what constitutes sexual abuse, particularly for boys. The result is that what constitutes abuse of boys in particular is often not acknowledged, leading to an under-reporting of incidents. Victimisers involved in the abuse of boys are likely to be treated more harshly than those involved with girls. This may be because there is a lack of acknowledgement in general in society that boys are sexually abused and when it is brought out into the open, the male victimiser is judged to be clearly in the wrong. On the other hand, there has been more than one occasion in which men who are accused of sexually abusing girls plead the seductiveness of a girl and her encouragement to them as mitigating factors. Judges have been known to criticise women involved in rape cases because of the way in which they dress and because of the time at night they have been out on the streets; the concept of 'contributory negligence' in sexually abused girls is an extension of this attitude.

Girls involved in incest cases often feel both responsibility for the incest and for the consequent disruption and unhappiness in the family. Fathers have been known to reinforce this and to have received sympathetic considerations in court, given that rules of evidence effectively weight the onus of proof in law against the young person. This attitude can also be reflected in the cases involving young people accused of soliciting. Girls can often expect to be fined or given a warning. Boys may be more likely to be subject to the possibility of some psychiatric assessment.

The study of Robert and Lois Pierce highlighted issues about treatment recommended by the courts. Male victims usually completed that treatment, but were likely to be seen for a shorter time than females. The authors suggest that this may be understood because of workers' assumptions that they would be less competent to deal with boys as opposed to girls, and that boys may be less disturbed by their experiences than girls. Both girls and boys are rarely seen in close temporal relationship to their assault because of the delay in identifying or reporting abuse. The widespread assumption that sexual abuse is more likely to involve girls, and the consequent failure to detect abuse of boys means that there is likely to be a greater time lapse for boys between abuse and any treatment being offered.

The effects of abuse

Statistics recording instants of sexual abuse suggest a ratio of 10:1 in favour of girls as opposed to boys. However, those dealing directly with young people would argue that this is an under-representation and that the ratio might well be closer to 6:4. Whatever the figures, it is clear that abuse occurs both to boys and girls.

Boys and girls are equally reluctant to report abuse. For boys it is the fear that they might be seen to be homosexual or that in some way their masculinity might be threatened, given the assumption in society that homosexual abuse does not happen. For girls, especially those abused in the family, there is a high level of anxiety of letting the secret out and not being able to control its dissemination.

For both girls and boys the fear of disclosure and the need to keep everything to themselves can be the worst aspect of the abuse, especially if it continues over an extended period. They feel guilty and feel they should be held responsible for whatever happens in the family. This is underlined by the fact that the young person, whether boy or girl, is far more likely than the victimiser to be taken out of the family when the secret is finally shared.

Girls are often found to take the dominant female role within their family. They may well often provide care for the other members and can be given a consultation role in decision making. They believe that their own, and their family's, survival depends on their willingness and ability to parent their parents. Boys abused in the family often show the same self-sacrificing attitude. Paradoxically, the sense of need and the reinforcement of self-sacrificing behaviour keeps both boys and girls in the role of a victim. Both exhibit a form of pseudo-maturity and feel they have to protect their family. As a result, assaults are likely not to be reported or when they are, not given the importance they deserve. Yet despite their responsibilities that both boys and girls feel they might have in their families, in reality they have little power, protection or security. Yet they are the ones that meet the emotional needs of the adults in their families.

Boys and girls suffer ambivalence and confusion from the effects of abuse. They both can experience pleasure from the abuse, a pleasure that leaves them with feelings of guilt that somehow or other they have consented and actually encouraged the encounter. Both need help to distinguish between genuine consent and involuntary physiological responses which may suggest consent.

It goes without saying that sexual abuse is traumatic for boys and girls and this trauma is coped with in a variety of ways that guarantee to bring the victims to public notice. So both boys and girls may well run away and truant from school. They may be withdrawn and depressed which is seen as a sort of internalised anger. On the other hand they can be extremely difficult to handle, being disobedient, rude and incorrigible. They can exhibit this as a form of externalised anger with everyone that comes into contact with them whom they feel do not appreciate why they are acting as they are. Some young people can be extremely violent both to themselves and to other people. They are unable to express verbally the shock, the disbelief and the terrible feelings of loss of childhood. They can only relieve the tensions that are tearing them apart internally by an external display of violence and aggression, sometimes done to others, sometimes to themselves, through forms of mutilation, drug/alcohol abuse or attempted suicide.

Young people experience a loss of self-esteem and self-worth. They feel bad about themselves, see themselves as unlovable, as damaged goods, deserving only a punishment. So they keep themselves as victims and become part of a cycle of abuse that may lead some youngsters into prostitution. This can be interpreted as a survival mechanism and as a counter-phobic reaction. It is a wish to push themselves into those areas that they fear most. For some girls especially it may be an attempt to bring a father or someone close to their family to justice. It can be a compulsive, repetitive process that has the effect of labelling the girl as provocative and a danger to men, giving even less credence to the origin of the abusive process. Both boys and girls may indulge in withdrawn, placating behaviour because of their feelings that they do not matter to anyone. This passivity sometimes results in increased violence and keeps them in the victim role. Girls may well comply with the victimiser because they feel that by so doing they will protect other children in the family.

The nature of abuse
Both boys and girls are molested in the same way and may experience fondling, masturbation, oral copulation and anal intercourse. Girls also experience vaginal intercourse but it is important to note that this is only a small portion of all abuse to girls. Both will be placed in positions where they have to take an active as opposed to a passive role.

Girls and boys are seduced by older men, though the experiences of boys are different in that they are primarily homosexual in nature. Girls and boys are likely to know their assailants, but those who molest boys are less likely to be family members. Some experts argue that boys may be less negative about their experiences than girls; certainly they are less likely to tell about them than girls.

Girls are more likely to be abused on their own compared with boys. Where boys are not abused alone, it is likely that others in the family will be involved, especially sisters. David Finkelhor[3] notes that boys abused on their own, as opposed to girls, or girls and boys together, are likely to be victimised by someone under 25. He says that these cases will usually involve an older sibling, a baby sitter or a young adult in the neighbourhood. In general, where the family is concerned, males are more likely to be abused by young relatives, for example, siblings or cousins, and girls by older relatives, for example, uncles or grandfathers. Both boys and girls are prone to be assaulted within their own homes, but boys are more likely to be abused in public places and may well suffer a greater degree of physical injury.

David Finkelhor outlines some of the characteristics of young people abused by their parents. He says that girls tend to be older than boys at the time that the abuse is reported. His research shows that boys and girls abused by mothers are younger than those abused by fathers. Sons abused by fathers are likely to be discovered at a younger age than sisters. This, Finkelhor says, is explained by the fact that they may well be the younger brothers of older victimised sisters. Boys victimised by mothers are the youngest of all.

Supporting the victims

There are some basic issues that are common in the treatment and supports given to both boys and girls. Both have a poor sense of self and a feeling of disgust. There is a need to improve the individual's self-esteem. Part of this process is to help boys and girls differentiate between the act or acts that took place and their value as individuals.

Girls and boys are open to further abuse because their capacity to judge motives and intentions of others is damaged. They have tremendous feelings of self-doubt because of their belief that the abuse may have been partly their own fault. This may be reinforced if their account of the abuse is not believed. Hence the need to listen, to believe and to reinforce that belief constantly. In this context it is important to stress that the abuser is the one that is in the wrong, not the young person.

The ability to choose between right and wrong is impaired, yet both girls and boys do have a sense of injustice and can know instinctively what is right and what is not. The likelihood of promiscuity is quite high. Both girls and boys have learnt to barter with their bodies to survive and to have their basic needs met. This has to be explained to them as a consequence, not a precursor, of sexual abuse and as a logical, even predictable reaction to a destructive situation.

As sexual abuse is a question of a misuse of power by an adult over a child, it is important to make clear that all those with power do not necessarily abuse it. It is also important therefore that the young person understands and gives agreement to whatever procedures or supports that may be set in motion.

Some young people stand out clearly as those more likely to be abused in future life. It is important to work on those issues that highlight this trend. Unlike boys, as girls become older they do not necessarily become more capable of physically warding off abuse. The impact of learning sexualised behaviour and responses, and of the victim role, at an early age can result in patterns of behaviour and language which attract further abuse. Particular help is needed to manage these destructive behaviours and to enable young people to recognise them as such.

Young people need help to cope with some of the more powerful flashbacks they experience. It is hard for them to explain their feelings that the abuser is present in the room and can almost be seen and touched. It is particularly difficult for them to speak about it because of their fear that adults may believe they are crazy. At the same time, the adult has to help the child distinguish between reality and fantasy and to take control of the situation, without underestimating the very real fear that is being experienced. In this context some young people will be totally dependent and feel unable to control their lives ever again. On the other hand, others will decide never to depend on an adult. Both approaches lead to difficulties, especially the ability to make safe relationships with others.

Boys and girls do wonder if they can ever have a proper loving relationship, because 'sex' can never be 'nice'. Girls in particular may feel forced to avoid sexual activities because the images they have about them are so powerful. There is the danger later on that images of their partners and their abusers will become fused, especially where a woman is unable to tell her partner of a previous history. The result may be a continuation of the abusing situation in the marriage. Others will use their bodies to get things because this has been their experience. In those cases their bodies and their feelings are remote from them as individuals and they will need support to remedy that situation.

Conclusion
Young people who have been abused will need to be put back in touch with their own personal power and positive potential. Both boys and girls may well have severe difficulties in adjusting in later life. There are some who would argue that this is not so much due to the abuse, but to the low level of parental support in the homes of such young people. Family environment they argue is a significant factor in the compilation of treatment programmes.

There is also the argument that challenges work with abused young people based on the family dysfunction model. The feminist viewpoint endorses the notion that the child is not to blame for the abuse and that the responsibility lies with the abusing adult. It argues that abuse is the product of patriarchal culture in which men hold the power in relation both to women and to children. This argument says that child sexual abuse is an abuse of male power and is part of the spectrum of general abuse committed by males in society. In this context treatment programmes would then view family rehabilitation as only one possible outcome rather than its primary goal.

References

1. Beverley James and Maria Nasjleti (1983) 'Treating Sexually Abused Children and Their Families: Consulting Psychologists'. Press Inc.
2. Robert & Lois Pierce (1985) 'The Sexually Abused Child: A Comparison of Male and Female Victims'. Child Abuse & Neglect' Vol.9, pp.191–199.
3. David Finkelhor, (1984) 'Child Sexual Abuse: New Theory in Research'. Free Press, New York.

Sexually abused boys: some considerations for white carers

■

BRENDAN O'MAHONY

Issues of race have not been high on the agenda of the boys' group. The group has had no representative from black or ethnic minority communities and it was only at the penultimate meeting that issues of race were discussed. As a consequence what follows in this paper is very limited because of the lack of time necessary to conduct proper research. This paper, written by a white male professional, aims to raise some of the issues involved and to emphasise that these issues have to be very high on the agenda for white workers when the care and treatment of sexually abused black young men is discussed.

There is a clear need to find out what statistics are available on the numbers of young black men who are abused. Such statistics would enable us to see whether there are significant differences between young black men and their white counterparts. In particular, if figures show that there are significantly less young black men coming forward who have been abused, that would then raise questions about what is preventing young black men from being able to disclose the abuse and receiving the help and support that they need.

There is no doubt that there can be certain myths held in the white community about the way in which Afro-Caribbean or Asian families bring up their children. There is a belief among white people that the patterns of black child-rearing are far more strict and that the use of physical or corporal punishment is quite excessive compared to that in white families. Having made assumptions about different attitudes to *physical* abuse, questions are sometimes raised about the potential for different attitudes to sexual abuse. White staff have to be wary of the unspoken thought, namely, that black people in general abuse their youngsters.

Assumptions around how black people live and their child-rearing practices by white therapists or carers can so easily be detrimental to diagnosis and treatment. This prejudice has a clear historical context, where black people have been seen as inferior, having attributes akin to a sub-human species. There are many examples of this in our history not least the unfounded and completely unfair assertion of the last few years, that somehow or other the HIV virus was a Central African problem, a 'black plague' that has been given to the white race. These may well be disturbing thoughts for white people, but an acknowledgement of cultural and historical racism is an essential element in any support that is given to a young black person who has been sexually abused.

The central issue in all this for white staff is to challenge in themselves and in the rest of their team any assertion that somehow or other white people and black people are not equal, are not the same, and that the former 'deserve' better treatment than the latter. In practice this means looking closely at the nature of the support and treatment offered to young black people. It is not so much the intention that is at fault. Therapists and carers are motivated to give young people the best possible service. It is in outcomes and the effects upon young black people that treatment can sometimes be found wanting.

Initially the therapist will be rightly concerned with helping a young black person with his distress and the immediate circumstances surrounding the abuse. However, the dynamic of racism will become more relevant as the therapeutic process develops. The issue of the abuse of adult power, but also the abuse of white adult power and the devisiveness and destructiveness of racism, should be very much a parameter of the service that is offered. The young black person may not appreciate these issues initially and it is right that the procedure that is adopted should be similar for every young person, namely, that this is an abused child who has suffered the abuse of adult power. However, as the treatment and support for a young black person who is abused continues, the issue of the abuse of white power in his life will become more relevant and will be of particular importance if the abuse has been carried out by a white person. The impact may not be immediate, but it will certainly have an effect later on. It is very important that the therapist is able to manage this area of the therapy very skillfully.

Thus, as part of the support to a young black lad who has been abused, the social and historical context of being black in British society is very important. For staff it is important to recognise the implicit undertones that white people have about what it is to be black in this society. The racist nature of these undertones has to be recognised by white staff if they are not to interfere with the work that they wish to carry out with and on behalf of the young person.

In an ideal world, the carer and/or supporter of the young black lad who has been abused would in the immediate aftermath of the disclosure be a black person. This would then counter directly some of the issues that a white worker faces trying to work through this disclosure with him. A black worker can offer support and in some senses make the situation 'normal' for the black lad because he or she will offer no long-term threat. Where a white carer undertakes the support and treatment initially because there is no black therapist available to provide a choice of therapist, there will be a need for professional supervision not only in the area of post-abuse therapy but also in relation to issues about race. This will obviously need to be undertaken within an agreed framework of confidentiality.

Part of the context that young black people have is the feeling, common to all those who have been abused, whether white or black, that it is their fault. However, for a black lad it is also about the fact that it is his fault because he is black. Offering an abused young black person, wherever possible, the choice of a black therapist or carer will mean that he can see around him immediately a supportive environment that upholds that which is good about being black.

Issues of race have to be high on the agenda for white staff in the treatment that they plan for young black lads that have been abused. White therapists have to be aware of their own racism. They must recognise that, while the good that they wish to undertake with and on behalf of the young person may not be discriminatory in intention, in practice, if issues of race are not taken into account, then the outcome could be clearly just that. Hence it is essential to be sensitive to a young black person and to raise as appropriate how that young person feels about being black in his situation.

Being abused is about having no choice. An essential part of any therapy is to restore choice to young people. To young black people it is also about making doubly sure that they are offered equality of opportunity and support. In that context issues of race are central to diagnosis and treatment.

Key issues for managing adolescent sexual behaviour in residential establishments[1]

■

BRENDAN O'MAHONY

Working with young adolescents in residential care is fraught with difficulty. The local authority, a statutory parent, faces all the dilemmas of a parent with children at home, yet also has to recognise the position of the natural parents and of the professionals, some of whom will come from voluntary bodies, who undertake the day to day care. All will have the interests of the young person at heart, yet all can disagree fundamentally on how particular situations should be approached and managed.

The management of sexual behaviour is not always clear-cut. Staff working in residence need to work out what constitutes sexual morality for a young person and how to achieve parental control between themselves, the referrer and the natural parents. Attempts by staff within the residential setting to lay down a code of sexual ethics and to control relationships both in and outside the unit in a manner that is fair and consistent, can often be interpreted as punishing and unrealistic by those outside. On the other hand, what a referrer might put forward as a flexible and realistic policy, is often interpreted as inconsistent and confusing by those that have to implement it on a day to day basis.

Problems can arise when a field-work agency expects a residential provision to change their established value systems to meet objectives set by those with no residential responsibility or experience. Residential staff may be unwilling or unsure how to tackle issues around sexual

---

1. Paper delivered to the Training Advisory Group on the Sexual Abuse of Children at the National Children's Bureau, Wednesday, 19th April 1989.

relationships, especially those that may involve overt acting out of homosexual or lesbian behaviour, or which may have violent, pseudo-sexual overtones.

It is often difficult in this context for the referrer and residential carer not to become part of the family dynamic and family struggle that has been instrumental in bringing the young person into care in the first place. The danger of a 'divorce' between the caring parties is real and they have to work hard to stay together and agree a common course of action.

There is a clear need therefore for written policies to be available in Social Services and in residential establishments about sexual relationships for young people in care. Is an expectation of total abstinence for young people realistic or possible? On the other hand, what boundaries need to be drawn? What exactly constitutes a sexual relationship?

Carers need guidelines in their approach to heterosexual and homosexual (including lesbian) behaviour among young people. They need to be clear whether there are or whether there ought to be differences in attitudes towards those young people in care who are under sixteen and those who are over that age. If there are distinctions to be made then these need to be clarified and their effects on other residents thought through.

Guidelines are necessary to help carers cope with relationships between consenting peers of the same age and sex. Distinctions need to be made between what is adolescent experimentation and what seems to be a continuing sexual relationship. The effects of any sexual relationships between peers of the same or different sex on the rest of the residential unit need to be clearly outlined and practice issues discussed. Staff have to know what limitations are placed on a young person's sexual development becauses he or she is in residential care, who is responsible for their implementation and what supports there will be when conflict arises.

Guidelines are also necessary for carers in their management of relationships between peers of the same age and sex where one peer is dominant. They need to ask whether one young person should be excluded from residential provision for the good of the whole. Then there is the thorny issue of how best staff can manage a relationship between a young person and an adult outside of the unit. They need to ask whether there are different approaches if the relationship is one between the same sex or one between different sexes.

What are the implications in all this for staff? What particular supports are needed by those who work in residence? They often may be relatively young and inexperienced workers, closer in age and thought to those they care for. Perhaps too much at times is expected from residential carers without enough formal training being given to them. Managers need to decide in this area how far young adults working in residential care need help to understand their own development as sexual beings without infringing upon their personal liberties. Structures that are confidential and supportive must also be available for those staff for whom working with abused young people may awake issues about the possible abuse in their own childhood. Likewise, clear procedure must be available to enable young staff to disclose any abuse of young people by other residential staff, especially those who may be in positions of authority over them. There is a danger that such secrets can be held in common by a residential staff group who can be too afraid to disclose a fear of the consequences on themselves. In this context they can mirror the silent suffering of those they are charged to care for.

The issue of a young person's sexual development is a sensitive one. It is important that where appropriate parents should be consulted and communicated with. Often action has to be taken quickly by residential staff. In such situations staff should be clear how far decisions can be delayed long enough for all parties to be consulted without detriment to the promptness of the action that needs to be taken. Carers work in an environment where external value systems may be changing. Managers have to be very clear how these changes can be implemented effectively for the good of the individual young person and the unit as a whole.

Every residential unit should have a written statement or agreement that outlines the extent and limit of its responsibility for intervention where abuse, whether it is physical, sexual, emotional or racial, may be suspected. In particular the decision-making process and a named contact person must be clearly outlined. Residential units should also have a clear statement setting out how a child protection approach may be adopted within the context and overall philosophy and practice of the work. Training should be given to all residential staff to ensure that they are able to identify and deal with disclosures of abuse by young people within the residential context. Regular supervision on this aspect of the work, opportunity to further training and a constant review of recorded information are all essential if the residential worker is to look after the welfare of a child or young person.

The issues raised in this paper are not ones that offer easy solutions, but they have to be on the agenda of all those who care for the young in a residential setting. Once such an agenda is worked through, a climate is created to allow young people the opportunity to disclose issues around sexual abuse in their lives. This is especially necessary for boys for all the reasons, personal and social, that inhibit them in particular from disclosure. It is important that all those with a responsibility for a young person in care, the local authority referrer, the residential workers and the parent, tackle these issues together both before admission to residence and as part of the on-going review of the caring service.

Sex rings

■

J. CHRISTOPHERSON

Recently a number of sex rings involving children have come to light, the largest of which may involve well over 100 children. As yet, however, relatively little work has been done to identify how best to help the children who have become involved in these rings. This article relies mainly on published material on a number of rings in Leeds, on Burgess *et al*'s study of American rings, and on discussions with staff involved in a number of large London rings.

Burgess *et al* (1984) have defined a sex ring as being composed of an adult perpetrator (or perpetrators) simultaneously involved with several children who are aware of each other's participation in sexual activity. Although technically they would be covered by this definition, some of the most publicised rings in the United Kingdom, such as the one at Congleton are largely outside the scope of this article, since they involve largely or entirely children from one family, and the protection and therapeutic issues will be essentially those relating to chaotic families as described in 'Child Sexual Abuse Within the Family' (Porter R., 1984), albeit on a very large scale. The Nottingham case described by Dawson (1989) shares characteristics of chaotic families, in so far as all the victims, and all those criminally convicted in it, were from one family, but she describes how other pedophiles used to visit the house to take part in ritual and satanic practices, some of which were of a very sadistic nature, reminiscent of practices described in Burgess *et al*. and in Finkelhor *et al*'s 'Nursery Crimes' (1988).

Burgess and her colleagues described three types of sex ring: solo rings, where there was only one adult involved, transitional rings, where the adult has tried to exchange pornographic pictures of children and pressurise the children into the next level, the syndicated ring, which is a well structured organisation geared to recruiting children to provide pornography or other sexual services on a commercial basis. Wild (1987) in his research of 11 rings identified in Leeds, uses the phrase transitional ring to describe rings involving several adults, but did not find such a clear link with child pornography. In one very large London ring, much pornography was found, but it did not involve the boys in the ring. Another London ring involved boys in providing pedophiles with entertainment, both sexual and otherwise, which included having pairs of them fight, semi-naked, and gambling heavily on the winner.

There have been cases of syndicated rings, often linked with children's institutions such as the Kincora boys' home in Northern Ireland, or the McMartin Day Nursery in California. (Finkelhor and Williams 1988 p.27ff). It is sometimes alleged that individuals of great wealth or power are involved with these rings, or that extreme violence has been used to maintain secrecy. Possibly because of such rings' effectiveness at maintaining secrecy, it is very rare for such cases to come to light. The ring involving the young fighters came to light when questions were asked about the large amount of money one of the boys had at his disposal.

The perpetrators

Perpetrators are usually male, and may be of any age. Some have grown up in the ring and graduated from victim to perpetrator. On the other hand, one perpetrator in Wild's study was 82. They may meet the children through legitimate points of contact, such as school boys' clubs or scout troups. They may make a point of becoming friendly with the children's parents in order to win their trust. In one ring described by Wild, a man of over seventy acted as a childminder for several months while the registered childminder with whom he lived was in hospital, using the opportunity provided to abuse his charges. Such trust only makes it more difficult to believe allegations when they are eventually made. Often, however, new children will be recruited to the rings by the members themselves. Perpetrators may make elaborate plans to attract boys into the ring. Redding (1989) describes how Ken Martin, the principle perpetrator in the Brent ring ran a market stall full of boys' toys, such as train sets and cars, and equipped his living room with three computers.

In some cases, perpetrators may take time introducing the children to sexual acts. In one of the London rings, only a small minority of the boys had been involved in sexual activity. On the other hand in the Leeds rings, some of the girls only came on one occasion, and were sexually involved then. Sometimes the sexual activity may take place in front of other children, or indeed between them. In other cases a 'chosen' child may be taken away from the group for sexual acts to take place with the perpetrator. There may be 'bondage', sadistic or even satanic aspects to the abuse, which may lend credence to demands for secrecy.

Loyalty is maintained by threats or bribery, or the provision of expensive toys or outings to which the children might not otherwise have access. The London perpetrators described themselves as having been 'in love' with the boys. Redding (1989) describes how the men in the rings had an 'all consuming passion for boys', doing nothing but go to work and look for them.

The victims

Rings may be either mixed or single sex groups. In Burgess *et al*'s study, which did not claim to be a representative sample, half were made up only of boys, and half each of the rest were either mixed sex or all girl groups. In the Leeds rings, the vast majority of the victims were girls, while in London all were boys. Almost all the children in all the rings were white. The youngest children were four, although children from nine until early teenage would be more usual. In some cases children were able to leave the groups when they were about sixteen, possibly because they were no longer of interest to the perpetrators. In Leeds, as Wynne and Wild (1986) have found, many of the children were recruited by ringleaders, girls of between twelve and fourteen, and children were often members of more than one ring. Ringleaders also maintained group loyalty. When the perpetrator in one ring was imprisoned, the ringleader took her girls to another man, who had no previous recorded history of sexual abuse, and soon he too was identified as a perpetrator. In London, boys brought their friends from school or their siblings into the ring.

In the United Kingdom rings, most of the victims had other social problems. Some of the Leeds ringleaders had also been sexually abused within their own families. Boys in London tended to come from families where their needs were not being met. Several came from families which were known to social services departments, others were at a special school where one of the most active recruiters was a pupil. Some had attended the Child Guidance Clinic and many were already known to the Intermediate Treatment teams as being on the fringes of delinquency. As Cockrell and Hoffman (1989) point out, the boys may have needed and enjoyed the man's attention and thus feel deviant when the man is punished.

Burgess *et al* report that children did not feel exploited because they regarded the sexual activities as payment for the provision of the rewards they received from the perpetrators. Nonetheless many wished to break out of the ring and sought ways of reporting it to the authorities without being held responsible by ring members for disclosure. More commonly rings came to light for external reasons, such as reports by members of the public of large numbers of children going to the homes of unattached men, possibly at unlikely times of the day. One American ring even came to light when police stopped the perpetrator's car and found a young girl in the front seat with him. He had been having her fellate him as he drove. All the Leeds rings came to light when one girl assaulted the penis of a five-year-old boy for whom she was babysitting declaring that she was 'fed up with willies' (Campbell 1988, p.104).

The effects on children of involvement in rings before disclosure are similar to those caused by other forms of sexual abuse: genital complaints, somatic anxiety symptoms, deterioration of school performance and so on. On disclosure feelings may, according to Burgess *et al* (1984b), resemble acute post-traumatic stress disorder, with generalised nervousness, sudden preoccupation with the events, guilt at parents finding out (especially if telling them has been one of the threats used to maintain the ring) or fear about reprisals from the perpetrator or other group members, or ridicule from other friends or acquaintances. Where the ring has been centred on a legitimate group, such as a church choir or scout troup, then the publication of the name of the group may lead to the victims being effectively named publicly. In the longer term some of the boys show hypermasculine risk-taking behaviour such as weaving bicycles through traffic, or holding on to bumpers of moving cars. As is the case with other sexually abused boys some may fear they have been 'made' homosexual, but the majority do not.

Intervention
When a large ring is discovered, the scale of the police and social work involvement which will be necessary is considerable. As in any case of sexual abuse, children should be interviewed jointly by a police officer and social worker. In investigating one London ring it was necessary to set aside a team of 8–10 social workers to work exclusively on the case. Investigations may have gone on for many weeks to turn suspicions into hard evidence, and the initial 'raid' will need to be carefully planned. Professionals must understand the procedures of colleagues with whom they work. The police officer in charge of the investigation of one of the large 'family' rings commented on his amazement at the number of people who had to be informed by social services of what was happening, and that he had revised his view that social workers dragged their feet in such situations. Another danger to be borne in mind is that with so many adults involved in a ring, it may well be the case that members of staff of the intervening agencies may be part of the ring and may warn other members of the ring or even use their power to call a halt to the investigation. It is important therefore not to assume that all professionals in the agency can be trusted with information about the investigation. Furthermore such

investigations are extremely costly, and the police input alone to the Brent inquiry, involving as it did the setting up of a special incident room, cost £397,000.

Such a large operation will inevitably attract publicity, and a temporary helpline may be useful not only to give an opportunity for other members of the ring to come forward or for other perpetrators to be identified, but a positive spin-off is likely to be that agencies receive information about other rings. Any such helpline will also attract adults who were molested as children who can be directed to the appropriate voluntary or self-help agency.

Because of the pressure on children to protect the ring, interviews may need to be more challenging than would normally be the case with child abuse victims but the danger of contamination of witnesses must as always be borne in mind, especially as given the complexity of the cases and the numbers of witnesses and accused, it may be many months or even run into years before criminal cases come to trial. Ideally witnesses should be kept apart during the run-up to the trial, but with dozens of children involved, many of whom go to the same school or are members of the same family, this might not be practical.

Social services departments may be ambivalent about the level of involvement which may be appropriate for them. On the one hand members of such rings are clearly and definably at risk, and are likely indeed to be already known to social workers. On the other hand, in the cases discussed in this article they are not at risk of abuse from their own families, and to case conference over a hundred children would require a vast amount of scarce professional time. The compromise achieved in one London case was to case conference all the boys who had been subject to penetrative sex, all the boys aged ten or under, and any boys where the social worker was concerned for other reasons. In all fifteen case conferences were held.

Therapeutically the key objective is to break down the secrecy of the ring so that the children involved can talk about it and come to terms with it openly. One dramatic way of doing this is to assemble all the members of the ring, together with their parents and enough workers to counsel each family afterwards, and review what happened. Parents and children can then be helped to come to terms with what has happened, and to realise that the blame for what has happened lies with the abusers. Otherwise there may be a danger that ring members, especially if they are boys, may come to identify with the abuser, and go on to repeat the abuse.

It is generally felt that ring members may need groupwork to provide them with the companionship of agemates that was previously provided by the ring. However, the cohesion of the Leeds rings even after the perpetrators had been removed, suggests that another approach may be to infiltrate the ring with a non-deviant non-sexual leader, or leaders so that the members' needs can continue to be met by the group. Cockrell and Hoffman (1989) describe how, in setting up a residential period for twelve boys aged nine to fourteen, who were or were thought to be, involved in prostitution, they found that the boys all knew each other, despite the fact that they came from different areas, went to different schools and were of widely different ages. There was a strong element of secrecy within the group, and the boys communicated by sign language or innuendo. Eventually they allowed staff to overhear discussions of their sexual activities. Leaders need to be very clear in their role however, and very skilled groupworkers, given the likely behaviour of group members. Cockrell and Hoffman found the boys also to be very protective of each other, particularly towards men.

Without appropriate treatment, Burgess *et al* (1984b) suggest that only a minority of sex ring members will make a positive adjustment as defined by continued educational and emotional development and an ability to express anger about the abuser. Others will deny its significance, but still suffer some adverse effects on performance or adjustment. Still more may abuse other children or identify with the abuser. Effective intervention is therefore essential.

Bibliography

Burgess A. (ed) (1984) 'Child Pornography and Sex Rings'. Lexington Books, Lexington, Mass.

Burgess A. (1984b) 'Response Patterns in Children and Adolescents Exploited Through Sex Rings and Pornography'. American Journal of Psychiatry 141:5 pp.656–662.

Campbell B. (1988) Unofficial Secrets. Virgo, London.

Cockrell J. and Hoffman D. (1989) 'Identifying the Needs of Boys at Risk in Prostitution'. Social Work Today, 18.5.89.

Dawson J. (1989) 'When the Truth Hurts'. Community Care, 30.3.89.

Finkelhor D. and Williams L.M. (1988) 'Nursery Crimes'. Sage, Newberry Park.

Porter R. (ed.) (1984) 'Child Sexual Abuse Within the Family'. Tavistock, London.

Wild N.J. (1987) 'Child Sex Rings in Contest'. Child Abuse Review, Spring.

Wild N.J. and Wynne J.M. (1986) 'Child Sex Rings'. British Medical Journal Vol.293, pp.183–185.

Planning groupwork for boys

■

ANNE PEAKE

Many of the issues in planning groupwork for girls and boys who have been sexually abused are the same. Careful sequential planning is essential if the group workers are to be freed during sessions to concentrate on what the children have to say and on making appropriate responses to the children. Groupwork needs to take account of the fact that sexual assaults on children are an abuse of power and a betrayal of trust.[2] It does seem that there are differences in some of the circumstances in which boys and girls are abused and in the way children/adults view their abuse.[3] Much of this is undoubtedly a reflection of the ways in which society differentiates between the socialisation of boys and of girls, the different pressures on boys and girls not to tell about sexual assaults, and different attitudes in our society to the victimisation of boys/men and girls/women.[4,5] A comparison of groupwork for boys and girls would suggest that there are also additional ways in which boys and girls respond differently in groups.[6] Thus it would seem that the gender of the children from whom groupwork is planned, has implications for both the method and the content of the work. This paper aims to set out some of the aspects of method and content that merit discussion when one plans to run groups for boys.

Planning issues
The gender of the workers
As is the case for girls, the majority of those who sexually assault boys are men. Finkelhor suggests a figure of 86%.[7] So the majority of boys are sexually assaulted by the same sex adults who are known to them beforehand. So these significant adults in their lives are modelling domination and violation of small children. These may well be adults whom the boys have been told or expected to emulate. It has been suggested that decisions about the gender of workers should be made

recognising any treatment work in the field of child sexual abuse. Frosh suggests male professionals have little to offer in disclosure work but do have a part to play in treatment work.[8,9] Decisions made about the gender of worker for groups for boys need to take place in this context. Often there have been discussions about the gender of workers but these are usually in relation to groups for girls.[10] There needs to be a separate debate when groups are planned for boys. While there is no clear definitive outcome to the debate, the workers need to have the debate and to be clear about the advantages and disadvantages of the choice of workers. The following discussion points are set out to help stimulate the debate. For the sake of brevity the advantages are set out, the disadvantages are to an extent implicit in the advantages for one choice as opposed to another choice.

- Groupworkers of both genders:

(a) Children in groups are said to benefit from contact with adults who are able to model male-female co-operation.

(b) Children need a worker of the same gender as their abuser(s) so that they can 'work through' their trauma. Two such workers would be overwhelming.

(c) The world and the daily lives of the children consist of combinations of men and women, and groupwork should represent this in the choice of workers.

(d) There are too few groupworkers able and/or willing to run groups for it to be practical to choose staff on the basis of gender.

- Groupworkers who are both female:

(a) Children deal better with past experiences of abuse and trauma if they can have 'an island of safety' – away from adults of the same gender as their abusers – on which to work out their feelings.

(b) Given a choice, abused children prefer female workers.

(c) It is important boys see women who provide positive, competent and sympathetic models.

- Groupworkers who are both male:

(a) Boys need alternative models of non-abusing, caring male adults.

(b) Boys need men to empathise with them if society is to break down the usual male socialisation pattern, ie. that men don't talk about feelings and are competitive.

(c) Women have difficulties in managing groups of boys, particularly teenagers and particularly tackling topics such as sex education and sexuality.

Even when one's plans for work with groups do not allow for a choice of workers on the basis of gender, a discussion of the advantages and disadvantages of the gender of the workers for the boys sensitises workers and places gender on the agenda for planning.

Grouping the boys
As with girls, the boys will have different treatment needs according to their ages, their ethnicity, the identity of their abusers, the circumstances of their abuse, the level of family belief and support.

The very difficult fact that some boys sexually assault others, both boys and girls; and that a proportion of these have themselves been sexually abused, means that there are issues in grouping the boys other than age, development, and the fact of their abuse. Often the numbers of boys referred for groupwork are fewer than the numbers of girls. In addition, the resources for groupwork with sexually abused boys are often fewer. Usually in any one Authority the first group to be set up is one for girls, and the majority of those workers willing to undertake groupwork with sexually abused children are women. In the face of small numbers and limited resources, a discussion about the basis for grouping boys other than age may seem an academic one. However, the different circumstances of the abuse and the presenting behaviour of boys in the following groups are such that workers ignore the issues at their peril, and more particularly at the peril of some of the boys!

(a) Boys who are assaulted by adults in their families or known to them or their families beforehand.

(b) Boys who are assaulted as part of a sex ring either with other boys or without knowing of the other boys. They need to be helped to deal with the organisation between adults who do this, the level of money involved, and the use made of pornography in our society.

(c) Boys who have been abused and who have gone on to abuse others. Arguably these boys could only be included in groups for abused boys if the level of supervision is high and the nature of their offending is short lived and completely known.

(d) Boys who sexually assault others but have no known history of themselves being the victim of child sexual abuse. Some may argue that for these boys treatment and the grouping of them will depend to a large extent on their ages. What is clear is that this group of boys cannot be properly catered for with groupwork, the content of which is geared to experiences of being the victim of abuse. The problem of boys who offend sexually raises different treatment goals.[11] Motivating the boys to face the groupwork process and managing a group of the boys to stay on task and not develop a tone in the group which reinforces behaviour, ie. boasting or seeking to shock/outrage the workers, needs planning and a special groupwork curriculum.[12] I would further argue that unless the following is addressed one should not plan to group these boys at all:

(i) There is always an extent to which those who refer sexually offending boys expect treatment to reduce the likelihood of recidivism. The referring professional and the group worker need to confront this and be explicit about how far this is likely to be an outcome, how it will be measured, and how will the issue of accountability of group workers for the work done in groups be squared with levels of recidivism.

(ii) There needs to be a societal context to work with offending boys which places responsibility clearly where it belongs, with the offender. If offending boys do not know this, then they will all too quickly rationalise their behaviours in ways which minimise the impact of what they have done, in very much the same ways as do adult sex offenders.[13,14] If they don't face their responsibility for their offending behaviour then the likelihood that they may in the future be free to recognise what may be their own history of being an abuse victim is reduced. Often their capacity to recognise their own past victimisation is hindered by society's unclear and confused reaction to their offending. I would suggest a helpful societal context for these boys is one in which their behaviour is not explained away as curiosity or exploration, but as a specific juvenile offence recorded as such. Such an approach makes society's view about sexual assaults a clear recorded measure of an individual boy's behaviour and whether this is improving or deteriorating over time.

(iii) A vital starting point to any work with these boys, individually or in groups, needs to be from a measure of the extent to which a boy's admission of his behaviour matches up with the account of the assault by the victim. If there is a huge disparity then workers need to question whether the work will only reinforce the offending boy's denial/minimising of his behaviour and reinforce his view of himself as in charge – even over the content of treatment work.

There needs to be a discussion of the treatment needs of the boys in these very different circumstances of abuse. It is unlikely to be helpful to put these four groups of boys together in the same group. It may well be after discussion workers decide that some individual work or work in small groups can be followed by perhaps grouping boys abused by known adults with boys who have been abused in sex rings, and perhaps abusing boys whose offending behaviour is very limited and who have a known history of being abused.

However, it is inadvisable to include juvenile offenders with no known history of victimisation with any of the boys already mentioned.

However, in grouping the boys consideration needs to be given to ensuring that no one boy is alone in the group in terms of the circumstances of his abuse: for example, boys abused by more than one person, a boy abused by a woman, etc. Similarly, workers need to see that the ethnic group of each child does not become a factor which isolates a boy: for example, having only one black boy in a group or having several black boys with white workers, etc.

Content issue
There are specific topics which should form a core of any content of groupwork for sexually abused children. These include: families, sex education, why children can't tell, abusers, what happens when children do tell, the short and long term consequences of abuse.[15] It is important in each topic to develop the content with specific reference to gender for both boys and girls. Ways this can be done for boys could include the following:

Families
There needs to be a specific reference to family roles with regard to gender. Stereotypes about gender differences in parent roles need to be examined and alternatives presented. Actively involving the boys in a critical survey of advertisements is one way to develop this idea.

Sex education
All sexually abused children need clear positive sex education which is able to deal with issues of pleasure, power, relationships, and sexuality. Work with boys needs to confront these issues very directly in ways which do not undermine the boys' sense of self but do tackle the abuser's behaviour. It is important to stress to the boys that it is the imbalance of age, size, power, and understanding, which underpin the abuse in its context of secrecy, making clear that sex used to compensate for one's own inadequacies, to dominate others, and without the consent of equals, will always be abusive.

Why children can't tell about sexual abuse

It does seem that fewer boys than girls are able to report and/or are recognised as the victims of child sexual abuse. It is helpful to children to give them some insight into the pressures on children not to tell, and so for boys including the specific reasons boys can't tell.[4,5]

Abusers

Boys are mainly abused by the same sex adult and this has obvious ramifications for the boys' development as adult sexual beings. Workers would need to prepare additional material which would permit the boys to consider options for themselves, for example, a group effort aimed at defining a non abusing male parent role.

What happens when children do tell

The response of agencies such as Social Services and Child Guidance Clinics to the warning signs of abuse in girls has encompassed the hypothesis of abuse and can offer both assessment and treatment resources. The warning signs of abuse in boys can be more difficult to contain and explain. Agencies have been slow to recognise the aggressive and sometimes sexual acting-out behaviours of boy victims. Such behaviours draw out the Police and Social Services in their containment roles in which there are often few assessment and treatment resources, and more punitive approaches.

The short and long term consequences of abuse

Few adult men survivors of child sexual abuse are prepared to tell their stories and to discuss the short and long term consequences of them of being abused. Often the media and the literature on the abuse of boys highlight two major consequences, both of them extremely negative. Firstly, the proportion of adult sex offenders who were victims of abuse as children is often quoted, 75–80%.[16] Secondly, the cycle of child/adult victim is said to be evidenced by the phenomenon of some sexually abused boys going on to be male prostitutes, 'rent boys'. It needs to be made clear to public and professionals alike the dangers of drawing generalised conclusions on the basis of 'abnormal' population samples. Certainly, given this impression in the press and some journals, workers with boys' groups need to present a credible third alternative: that of men becoming survivors of childhood sexual assaults, going on to live successful and non abusive work and personal lives. The absence of materials such as videos, survivors' accounts, makes this particular topic of the work difficult to present. It is nonetheless a crucial part of the content.

Issues related to particular groups of boys

There may well be additional topics/themes which will need to be woven into the content of groupwork for boys. These will be related to the particular circumstances of the abuse of the boys who are abused in sex rings, will need to talk about the networks of adults who victimise children, the link between the children's experiences and money made by adults, and the nature of the violence/pressures not to tell.[17]

Organisation issues

Linking groupwork with the family process

It is important that the groupwork is linked in the work with families of the boys. If this is not done, then families can be resentful of the care and attention paid to the boys and/or misunderstand the aims of the work, and so undermine the work in the group. Again the circumstances of the boy's abuse may well have implications for the way in which the group work is linked in to the family process. For example, when the group is dealing with boys abused as part of a sex ring there may be an issue of only being able to group the boys and link with the families once a decision has been made about prosecution and the case heard in court. As some cases can involve sex rings of over one hundred children, cases may well take a long time to go to court. A second example would be when the group is primarily for juvenile sex offenders, where some of the boys have minimised their offending behaviour and not disclosed earlier victimisation. These boys may well work to destroy links between the group workers and those working with their families. As more is learned of the boys' behaviours and past histories, this may present problems in terms of the extent to which the family resources can be mobilised to support the boys in the group.

Evaluation

An assessment of the effectiveness of any treatment plan should be part of the process. The evaluation of groupwork needs to be accessible to other professionals, including those who refer children to groups and non abusing parents. If the evaluation is accessible then it permits comparisons between different methods.[6] The effectiveness of groups is particularly a priority with regard to offending boys[11] and boys who have been abused together as part of sex rings who miss what they perceived as the gains of their victimisation.

References

1. Peake A. (1989) 'Planning and Organising Groupwork for Older Children (11 years upwards)'. Children's Society, London.
2. Furniss T., Bingley-Miller L. and Van Elburg A. (1988) 'Goal Oriented Group

Treatment for Sexually Abused Adolescent Girls'. British Journal of Psychiatry, 152, pp.97–106.

3. Baker A. and Duncan S. (1985) 'Child Sexual Abuse: A Study of Prevalence in Great Britain'. Journal of Child Abuse and Neglect, Vol.9, pp.457–467.

4. Peake A. (1989) 'Issues of Under Reporting the Sexual Abuse of Boys'. British Psychological Society DECP Occasional Papers Child Sexual Abuse, p??.

5. Peake A. (1989) 'Why Children Can't Tell About Sexual Abuse And How Some Do Tell'. Children's Society, London.

6. Peake A. (1987) 'An Evaluation of Groupwork for Sexually Abused Adolescent Girls and Boys'. British Psychological Society, Division of Educational and Child Psychology. Occasional Papers, Vol.4, Nos.3 & 4, pp.189–203.

7. Finkelhor D. (1984) 'Child Sexual Abuse'. Free Press.

8. Frosh S. (1987) 'Issues for Men Working with Sexually Abused Children'. British Journal of Psychotherapy, Vol.3, pp.332–9.

9. Frosh S. (1988) 'No Man's Land?: The Role of Men Working with Sexually Abused Children'. British Journal of Guidance and Counselling, Vol.16, No.1.

10. Gottlieb B. and Dean J. (1981) 'The Co-therapy Relationship in Group Treatment of Sexually Mistreated Adolescent Girls' in 'Sexually Abused Children and their Families'. (Edit) Mrazek P.B. and Kempe C.H. (1981), Pergamon Press.

11. Ryan G., Lane S., Davis J. and Isaac C. (1987) 'Juvenile Sex Offenders: Development and Correction'. Journal of Child Abuse and Neglect, Vol.11, No.3, pp.385–395.

12. Smets A.C. and Cebula C.M. (1987). 'A Group Treatment Program for Adolescent Sex Offenders: Five Steps Toward Resolution'. Journal of Child Abuse and Neglect, Vol.11, pp.247–254.

13. Wyne R. 'Men Women and Rape'.

14. Snowden R. (1980) 'Working with Incest Offenders: Excuses, Excuses, Excuses'. Aegis' issue on Child Sexual Assault No.29.

15. Peake A. (1989) 'A Curriculum for Groupwork'. Children's Society, London.

16. Renvoize J. (1982) 'Incest: A Family Pattern'. Routledge and Kegan Paul.

17. Vander Mey B.J. (1988) 'The Sexual Victimisation of Male Children: a Review of Previous Research'. Journal of Child Abuse and Neglect, Vol.12, No.1, pp.61–72.

Group Therapy For Boys[1]

■

DR. TILMAN H. FURNISS

Being 'normal in context'

In the treatment of children who have been seriously abused, group therapy, together with family work, is the treatment of choice. Sexually abused children often define themselves entirely through their experience of abuse. They feel they are the only children to whom sexual abuse has ever happened. They may feel guilty, isolated and different from their peers. They often feel dirty and unloved and suffer from very low self-esteem. In a situation where all children are sexually abused, however, individual children cannot continue to define themselves solely through the abuse. In a group setting for sexually abused children, the individual abused child is not defined as special through their experience of sexual abuse because everybody else in the group has similar experiences. Children in such a setting can begin to discover aspects of their personality and areas of strength and potential in themselves and in other children in the group which had previously been buried under the self-definition through the abuse.

Within group sessions for sexually abused children, all children are 'normal in context' of the group. This makes it much easier to break the secrecy and isolation of the individual child. The self-help component in groups also counteracts the common feeling of uniqueness of their experience in the isolation of the sexual abuse of the individual child.

Therapy and protection work with children

The important differentiation between therapy and protection work with sexually abused children is often ignored. This distinction reflects the

---

1. This chapter was first published in slightly changed form in: T. Furniss (1989) 'Multiprofessional Management and Treatment of Child Sexual Abuse'. Routledge, London.

important difference between child sexual abuse as a human rights issue and as a child mental health problem. These two domains, although related, are quite separate in origin and in their requirement for response.

All sexually abused children need some protection work but not all need therapy to the same extent. All sexually abused children are to some degree confused about their experience as a result of the secrecy. They need permission and encouragement to talk about their sexual experience to provide some relief from their confusion. All children need some work to help to prevent further abuse. But not all sexually abused children are psychologically disturbed to a degree which requires therapy.

Although not all children are psychologically *disturbed*, all children are psychologically *affected* by the abusive experience. It is therefore paramount that sexually abused children are carefully assessed for psychiatric disturbance. Children who have been victims of less severe forms of abuse may need only short-term and structured prevention work. Other children may need intensive and long-term therapy.

Protection groups

Protection work and protection groups relate to the legal aspects of child protection and the need to prevent further abuse. Protection groups can be of much shorter duration than therapy groups. They can be more structured and directly educational in teaching children social skills and in dealing with the external aspects of secrecy.

Protection groups need to address the following seven areas in relation to secrecy and child protection.

1. Children need permission to break the secrecy and to communicate and talk openly about the abuse.

2. Children need help to find explicit sexual language to talk through an experience about which families do not communicate and for which children may not have a language to do so.

3. Children need to talk openly about the facts of their abuse and about their experience in order to prevent future psychological disturbance as consequence of the confusion about the abusive experience.

4. Children need to learn to recognise early enough different forms of approaches by adults which may indicate an intent to sexual abuse.

5. Children need to learn that it is important to find somebody who listens to them when they want to disclose further sexual abuse.

6. Children need to acquire the necessary skills to identify a Trusted

Person who will believe them if they feel threatened by renewed child sexual abuse.

7.   Finally children need to be able to refuse inappropriate physical or sexual contact. They have to learn to say 'No' if somebody tries to touch them in a sexualised and frightening way and they need to know what to do in this situation.

The work on 'good touch' and 'bad touch' and on the children's 'own body' relates to this area. Protection work should teach children to become able to talk more openly about sexual abuse and should show them how they can protect themselves from further abuse and how they can find other people who will help them to do so. Structured weekly groups of 3–4 months can often cover the 7 areas of protection work in 8–12 relatively structured sessions. Protection groups can be *closed* groups with a relatively fixed programme and duration. Groups for protection work should become an integral part of the basic work of any child protection agency involved in statutory work with child sexual abuse.

Protection groups also have a therapeutic aspect when they help children to open up the secrecy and to talk about their experience. Conversely all therapy groups need to include coverage of the seven areas of protection work. Therapy and protection are not mutually exclusive or oppositional. They are complementary aspects of dealing with the consequences of child sexual abuse as a legal and health problem and as a syndrome of secrecy and addiction.

Structured short term protection groups are the group work of choice for young children who are not mature enough for the more complex processes of longer term therapy groups which fully use group therapeutic processes. In older children protection work and fully developed group therapy can be used according to the child's needs. All children can start in protection groups. Older children who need more can then join therapy groups. With young children individual work or work with the mother-child dyad is more appropriate.

Where children have not only become confused but are also psychiatrically disturbed and traumatised by severe or long-term sexual abuse, group work must focus beyond the child protective aspects and beyond the aspects of confusion through secrecy on more fundamental aspects of child mental health. Therapy groups may need to start with structured sessions, followed by more open sessions addressing specific psychotherapeutic needs of the children involved. Therapeutic methods of change will have to be employed and therapy groups will need to run for much longer than protection groups.

The clear distinction between protection work and therapy is based on differences in the children's needs, on differences in aims and goals and on differences in techniques and skills required. The clear distinction is not least necessary because of the growing number of sexually abused children and the very different resource implications for short-term protection groups and longer-term therapy.

Group structures of therapy groups

Therapy groups can be *closed* or slow, *open* groups. In slow open groups the membership can build up over time and new children join in during ongoing therapy. Slow open groups have the advantage that they are easier to start because they need fewer referrals initially. It is quite possible that a proper group process can be initiated in a group with only three children. In slow, open groups long-standing group members can be very effective in helping newcomers to break the secrecy and to talk about the abuse. Slow, open groups can also more easily cater for the different time span which different children need in therapy. The disadvantage of slow, open groups lies in the frequent interruption of the ongoing therapeutic process through the arrival of newcomers and when other children leave the group.

The advantage of closed groups lies in the shared starting and ending point which makes the therapeutic process much more homogeneous and coherent. The disadvantage lies in the need for sufficient numbers of referrals of children at about the same time who are about the same age and at about the same stage of psycho-social development. In addition closed groups cannot cater for divergent needs in the length of therapy. In closed groups children who need longer therapy may have to move to new groups.

Who can join the group?

The goal-oriented nature of the groups means that only sexually abused children can be eligible. This can sometimes pose problems when siblings have not themselves been sexually abused but are nevertheless disturbed by their experience of sexual abuse of a sibling and by the underlying dysfunctional family process. Disruption and distortion of the specific group process can result from the inclusion of children who have not been sexually abused themselves, and this should make direct experience of child sexual abuse the pre-condition for group membership. Disturbed children who have been affected by the sexual abuse of a sibling but who have not themselves been sexually abused may be offered a combination of individual and family therapy instead of joining the group. There may be exceptions, however, where a sexually abused child and a non-abused sibling who has known about the abuse and who has been severely affected may both join the same group. This can especially be the case when the non-abused sibling is older, closely involved with the sexually abused child and has known or seen the abuse, with consequent feelings of responsibility for not having prevented the abuse and for not having protected the sibling.

Mixed or single sex?

In the combination of group therapy and family therapy, both mixed sex groups and single sex groups have shown to be helpful. Specific sex related experiences and psychological processes can be more easily dealt with when boys and girls have separate groups. This may not be so relevant in groups for younger children. It certainly holds for adolescent groups where issues of full sexual maturation pose very sex-specific problems. Although it is helpful if children in the group are of comparable age and stage of psycho-social and psycho-sexual development, mental state and the degree of disturbance should only be limiting factors in extreme cases when the group process is too much disrupted in the presence of the excluded child.

Size and duration of group

Groups of five to eight children seem to be the optimal size. With less than five children, the group process can become too diluted. If only one or two children are absent or are in a withdrawn state the other children and the therapists have to work very hard to maintain the group process. The complex life situation of many sexually abused children after disclosure often leads to failure to attend sessions. Stressful periods in the family process when parents are less co-operative and when children are less willing to attend, together with problems in the professional network for children in care can prevent attendance of the group. A group number larger than eight makes it difficult to give each child appropriate time, space and attention during the group session. We need to make sure that individual children in the group have enough time and space to deal promptly with crisis issues whenever they arise, bearing in mind that sexually abused children often experience many environmentally and family induced crises during therapy.

Working with children in weekly sessions of one hour's duration seems to be optimal. Longer sessions often overstretch children's attention span and can psychologically be too heavy for children and therapists. In addition it is always easier – and not harmful to the group process – to negotiate longer sessions than to struggle with over-exhausting lengthy meetings or cutting down the duration.

The therapist(s)

It can be of great advantage to have a therapeutic couple of a female and a male therapist who can represent the respective female and male gender aspects and who can model important functions of co-operation and mutual support in the parenting couple. The disadvantage of a couple lies in the increased danger of splitting of the therapist couple by the children. Splitting of the therapist couple is an important problem in any group therapy. The danger of splitting is vastly increased in group work of child sexual abuse as a result of the specific gender issues for the therapists and due to the enhanced ability of sexually abused children to split adult couples who have parenting functions.

The contentious issue of the gender of the therapist in groups run by a single therapist requires differentiation and not distancing. Male therapists can, as much as female therapists, run both boys' groups and girls' groups. The importance is that male and female therapists need to be aware of different gender-specific advantages and disadvantages for both sexes.

The success of therapy in groups with single therapists depends above all on the female or male therapist's awareness of these gender issues and on her or his own personal ability to deal with the specific problems of child sexual abuse as a person himself or herself. The very personal attitude of the therapists and their skill determines whether they are able to use fully the advantages and to minimise the disadvantages of their gender in relation to the specific gender related problems in the therapy of sexually abused children. I myself have seen some children who refused to see a male therapist out of fear of repetition of the abusive situation. I have equally seen children who were too frightened to be treated by a female therapist as result of their experience of maternal rejection, non-believing, let-down or blaming for the abuse. Again ideology must take second place to problem-oriented professional differentiation.

Aims and goals in therapy groups

The basic aims and goals in group therapy for sexually abused children are directed at the children as individuals, as family members and as members of the peer group. The aims need to be adapted to specific group processes and communication structures according to the age and stage of maturation of the children in the group.

We have four main aims which are directed at the child as individual:

1. We try to help the children find a language to communicate about the abuse.

2. We teach sexually abused children about normal sexual development in the light of their often unexpected ignorance about basic sexual facts.

3. We try to help to rebuild their self-esteem.

4. Finally, we help children to develop a sense of choice about their lives, thus countering the sense of helplessness and victimisation they have experienced during the abuse.

We have three main goals in relation to parents and families:

1. Therapists working in couples need to reintroduce appropriate intergenerational boundaries. Male therapists can aim to give the children direct experience of non-abusing, non-secretive and non-threatening male adults. Female therapists can provide the experience of a reliable and trustworthy, though firm, female figure. Single therapists working on their own will aim at the same goals trying to represent both sides.

2. It is important to offer a different parenting model from that which the children know from their families and to provide the experience of two united therapists who work together and who do not allow themselves to be divided.

3. It is crucial to help the children distinguish between the reality of the abusing parent's responsibility for the abuse and the consequences of disclosure and their own feelings of responsibility, guilt and self-blame.

In relation to the children's peer group, sexually abused children need to work on three essential areas:

1. They need help to overcome the fear of isolation and to learn to talk openly about the abuse in front of their peers who had similar experiences.

2. Sexually abused children need to build or rebuild normal adolescent or pre-adolescent peer group relationships within the group first before they can develop normal peer group relationships outside.

3. Any sexualised behaviour must be addressed. Children need to become aware of unconscious sexualised messages they may give to others. They have to learn to desexualise interpersonal relationships with other group members and with the therapists. It is crucial therapeutically and in protective terms, that sexually abused children become able to relate in non-sexualising ways.

Methods and techniques in therapy groups

In therapy groups for sexually abused children we need to employ some specific methods and techniques in addition to those used in general group therapy which relate to specific aspects of child sexual abuse as a syndrome of secrecy. It is important for the individual child, and for the other group members, that each child at the beginning of the group tries to tell once openly what has happened to her in front of other group members and to hear from the other children themselves what has happened to them. It is also vital to deal with reality issues of sexual anatomy and explicit sex education. It is necessary to ensure that sexually abused children can name their anatomy and feel that they have permission to do so. Girls, especially, often feel physically damaged. If children complain about pains we need to be absolutely certain that they are not physically injured in reality before we deal with the many and frequent fantasies about internal damage. This is especially important for older girls who often fear that they will never be able to have children, as punishment for the abuse. The differentiated use of the following six techniques according to specific areas of work has been very helpful.

1. **Interpretation.** Interpretations should centre on the immediate process within the group and between the girls and the therapist.

2. **Direct teaching.** Teaching methods can provide important factual information about issues of sexual anatomy and sexual development and may need to include such topics as pregnancy prevention in groups for older adolescent girls and boys.

3. **Anxiety reducing group games.** Anxiety reducing forms of group games may be used to find the appropriate sexual language in the initial period of therapy and to address group issues which are otherwise too frightening. In order to find appropriate sexual language, at the start of the group, for example, children can write down on a piece of paper, secretly, different names for different sex organs. These are then put into a box. The box is then emptied on the table and the members of the group and the therapist will read out the names aloud. This little game deals with an area which is loaded with shame, embarrassment and anxiety in a way which quickly engages all group members in an often very relaxed and non-threatening way.

    When children in the group are too frightened the therapist may need to be the first person who starts reading out the names giving the children in the group permission to use open sexual language themselves. It also conveys the message to the group that the therapists can cope with explicit sexual communication in an appropriate way.

4. **Active physical intervention.** Therapists must be prepared to intervene actively and physically to contain children in situations of potentially dangerous acting out. Physical contact, especially by male therapists, is a very difficult aspect in treating sexually abused children and needs to be thought about extremely carefully. Appropriately used physical boundary setting however can be experienced as very anxiety relieving in self-destructive acting out in the group. The problem of physical contact and the protection or violation of physical integrity and boundaries can subsequently be verbalized as a central theme in the therapeutic process.

5. **Addressing non-verbal communication.** Drawing materials, plasticine and other materials should be provided to help the children to express themselves non-verbally when verbal communication is not yet available or proves too problematic. Putting things on paper can sometimes be very helpful to enhance the children's sense of reality about issues of sexual abuse which have often been secret and hidden from open acknowledgement for many months and years.

6. **Role play and video feedback.** Role play and, where available, video feedback are helpful tools to increase social skills and self-assertiveness as therapeutic and directly protective elements in therapy.

Special issues in groups for boys

In groups for young children boys and girls can be mixed. In late pre-puberty and in puberty gender issues and issues of sexual identity become important and adolescent girls and boys need to be seen in separate groups. The basic principles of group work outlined earlier in this chapter also apply to boys. We need to keep in mind that the common issues of victimization through sexual abuse are much more fundamental than gender specific differences. However, we need to keep the following nine gender specific points in mind when we deal with sexually abused boys:

1. Boys tend to find it very difficult to open up in groups and to talk about psychological problems. They can be very embarrassed towards women as a result of homosexual abuse.

2. Sexually abused boys may have experienced that male abusers have made repeatedly derogatory remarks about their mothers and about women in general. The abuser might have instilled feelings of hostility and denigration towards the mother and towards other women which can be reinforced by the boy's disappointment of not having been protected from the abuse.

3. In later adolescence boys may feel that they are expected to cope without help. Like male rape victims they might feel that their request for help is seen as a sign of personal weakness. Male stereotypes still play an important role, not only in relation to abusing but also in relation to victimisation.

4. Homosexually abused adolescent boys are in a different position towards their mother as the non-abusing parent than girls. In gender identification adolescent girls can turn to their mothers for help and support. Adolescent boys find it usually impossible to turn to their mothers as the non-abusing parent to talk about issues of sexuality and even less about homosexual abuse. The confusion about sexuality and sexual identity which is normal in adolescence is already confounded through the abuse. Sexually abused boys need to find a non-abusing male confidant to whom they can talk about the sexual aspects of the sexual abuse and about their gender-specific relationships to men and women. If such a therapeutic and protective paternal figure cannot be found the role of peer group relationships within the group becomes even more important.

5. Sexually abused boys are nearly always to some degree confused about their sexual identity. Fears of being homosexual are generally strong. Mixtures of pleasurable experiences and frightening abuse in the abusive interaction can add to the confusion. Some boys who have had very frightening experiences may fear that they had lost all masculinity. Boys who have been aroused during homosexual abuse need to deal with the real and at times strong aspects of homosexual tendencies which are induced through the abuse.

6. In addition to the topic of homosexuality issues of sex drive need to be addressed. Some boys fear total loss of sex drive and feel emasculated. Other boys may have learnt to find tension relief in compulsive masturbation. The abuse has taught them to find instant tension relief in sexualization of any form of anxiety and stress. This tendency can lead to the imagined or well-founded fear of boys becoming sexual abusers themselves.

7. Many sexually abused boys are frightened of becoming abusers themselves. It is essential to address this fear because a substantial number of sexually abused boys do become sexual abusers later in life with the abusive activity often starting in puberty. In fact, it is vital to keep in mind that adolescent boys might have *already* become abusers themselves. This risk is especially high when other children in the family have been abused as well. Although sexually abused

boys may assume victim roles we find more often a tendency to actively act out and to become abusers themselves.

A circular and self-reinforcing process leads to a real danger of becoming an active abuser. Homosexual abuse by father-figures prevents the boy from making adolescent relationships with girls in which he can re-evaluate his relationship to the opposite sex. The lack of normal adolescent experimenting leads to increased difficulty in developing open and positive relationships to girls. The more intense the sexualisation in the abusive relationship, and the less clarified the relationship with girls and women, the greater is the danger for the boy to find tension relief in sexual activities and in compulsory masturbation. The sexualisation of anxiety and frustration in the context of increasingly estranged or hostile relationships towards girls and women leads to the danger for sexually abused boys to become sexual abusers themselves.

8. In cases where boys are more vulnerable through absent fathers the abuser has often become a 'good uncle' figure. The attachment of boys to abusers can be very strong and they may feel that they are disloyal towards the abuser when they talk in the group about the abuse.

9. At the other end of the spectrum abused boys can become very aggressive towards the abuser. They often wish to harm him and are frightened of losing control in violent outbursts.

Therapists in boys' groups need to address the following eight aims and goals:

1. Adolescent boys need specific help to open up in the group, especially in the presence of women.

2. Sexually abused adolescent boys need to overcome gender stereotypes and need to allow themselves to ask for help in the group.

3. The group needs to address fears and tendencies of homosexuality as a result of homosexual abuse.

4. The group needs to address possible ongoing sexual abuse by the boys themselves and they need to address the fears of becoming abusers later in life.

5. The boys need to be able to talk openly about issues of tension relief. It is crucial to deal with any sexualization of tension relief.

6. The boys should be encouraged to talk in the group about their sexual fantasies and their masturbation fantasies in order to evaluate

abusive tendencies. As in the process of opening up other difficult areas of sexual abuse, therapists will need to give the boys explicit permission to communicate about their sexual fantasies by introducing the subject themselves in a normalising and anxiety-reducing way. It can be very helpful if the therapist opens up the topic by saying that all men masturbate and that everybody has sexual fantasies and that they might be very strange at times. It is very important that the therapist then gives an explicit example in an emotionally as neutral a way as possible.

7. The group needs to address the relationship and attitudes towards sisters, mothers and women in general. The ability to relate emotionally in a non-sexual way to girls and women is crucial for therapy and for prevention.

8. The group needs to help each boy to think about finding a non-abusing father figure to whom they can relate, to whom they might be able to talk about the abuse and with whom they can identify as boys and young men. It is often very difficult to find a trusting male figure for the boys and the group and the therapists might need to fulfil this role as well as possible.

Other aims and goals in boys' groups must be seen in the context of the general aims, goals and treatment process which is outlined earlier in this chapter. In some cases sexually abused boys will have already become adolescent sex offenders. The nature of sexual abuse as syndrome of secrecy and addiction requires that the boys take responsibility for abusing before their own victimization and abuse can be addressed. Otherwise the experience of being abused will be used by the adolescent sex offenders to avoid facing the responsibility for their own abusive behaviour.

Training for work with sexually abused boys

■

ANNE HOLLOWS & HELEN ARMSTRONG

The Boys Group, which produced the preceding papers in this publication, considered primarily the specific practice issues involved in this area of work. In this paper, written after the completion of the work of the Group, we have attempted to identify the key issues for trainers and managers of services to sexually abused children in preparing and training workers for their task.

The earlier papers in this publication have identified some of the specific issues which require consideration when working with boys who have been sexually abused. These issues arise from a number of sources; from the nature of the offence itself, the victim's responses and interpretations of that experience and broader societal attitudes to both victim and abuser. The differing patterns and characteristics of abuse of boys and girls are crucial in all this. The papers have also drawn attention to some of the differences in attitudes and assumptions of workers in a range of settings.

In the development of professional responses to sexual abuse it has to a large extent been assumed that most of those abused are girls. These papers state clearly that this is an incorrect assumption – in fact, an assumption which may itself hinder the detection of abuse among boys. Managers of services provided for children who have been sexually abused will have recognised from these papers that it will be important to adopt different strategies and responses to investigating and treating sexual abuse among boys. The task for the trainer is to identify how these specific issues can be addressed in the context of a sound training approach which relates working with boys to broader issues of working in sexual abuse.

In 'Good Enough Training' (Hollows, Armstrong and Stainton Rogers, 1989) the framework for and method of building an overall training approach for work in the field of child sexual abuse are identified. This includes the process of building up knowledge, skills and self awareness appropriate to the level of work required of the practitioner in her or his work setting. Training for work with abused boys needs to be built upon a foundation of sound training for work in sexual abuse generally. The training for work with boys will reflect many of the broad content areas of training for work with girls, but with a more focused attention to those aspects which require exploration for the more specific area of work.

The key areas for all training in work with sexual abuse can be organised under six main headings – knowledge, feelings and attitudes, skills, obtaining and using support, working together and developing critical abilities. It will be important also, as with any area of work, to be able to identify, select and use appropriate resources, as well as being involved in the appropriate development of services and resources where none exist. This model can be revised for any specific area of work within sexual abuse and indeed has application more widely in child care.

For work with boys who have been sexually abused the model needs to address specific content areas, including the following:

Knowledge
Context knowledge:
— reinforcement of knowledge of relevant areas of the law and inclusion of the context of recent legislation;
— revision of knowledge of local procedures;
— revision of knowledge on child development, with particular reference to boys.

Subject knowledge:
— knowledge of the specific activities likely to be included in abuse of boys;
— knowledge of the prevalence and patterns of abuse of boys as drawn from current research and practice (such as that incorporated in these papers);
— awareness of the impact of socialisation on the possible presentation of abuse of boys, its effects on victims and thus on indicators;
— knowledge of specific medical information, for example physical consequences of abuse, information on HIV testing etc.

Feelings and attitudes
— exploration of personal responses and attitudes to abuse of males by

males, and of males by females, with reference to age, relationship etc;

— exploration of attitudes to adolescent experiences of sex and to 'experimentation';
— consideration of the responsibility for drawing up professional guidelines for responses in this area;
— examination of impact of wider societal attitudes to homosexuality and their impact on victim and others;
— consideration of the way factors of race, ethnicity and culture impinge upon the experience of sexual abuse of boys and the victim's experience of professional intervention;
— consideration of issues of confidentiality.

Skills
— skills of communicating with boys including awareness of specific potential problems;
— skills in organising and running groups for abused boys;
— skills and professional strategies for addressing work with sex rings;
— skills in talking with parents and other adults about abuse of boys;
— skills in addressing responses of different ethnic, cultural and religious groups to the abuse of boys.

Obtaining and using support
Working with supervisor/consultant to ensure that:
— there is a shared and mutually accepted baseline of feelings and attitudes;
— reactions to new or unexpected situations can be shared and supported;
— local resources for therapeutic and support work with boys can be identified.

Working together
— training to work with other disciplines and professionals with a shared baseline of feelings and responses;
— work to raise awareness in local agencies, such as schools, of the potential abuse of boys and the need to be alert to its occurrence.

Developing critical abilities
Encouraging skills in reflecting upon and assessing own work, developing an ongoing awareness of societal attitudes to abuse of boys and an understanding of how this affects personal and agency response to abuse of boys.

Problem areas in training

There are two particular problem areas for trainers in this area of work. The first is the need to be particularly alert to the potential difficulty of some aspects of training in this area and to the likelihood of strong feelings and possibly disagreements arising in the training group. More than in any earlier training which participants have undertaken, they will be required to confront their own attitudes to sexuality. We address some of these issues in detail in 'Good Enough Training' and suggest some strategies for dealing with the management of conflict and powerful emotions in training. It will be important for trainers to consider this aspect with care and plan accordingly.

The second problem is that training for work with boys is often (though not always) introduced as a response to the discovery of a major incident of abuse of boys such as a sex ring. At this stage the swift development of a package of training which may be out of sequence with other training initiatives is often required because there is no other course of action open to the agency. In this situation, training for work with boys will have to identify and tackle the deficit of training needs in the more general issues of work with abused children.

Context issues for training

Training will need to be, to some extent at least, focused on the specific work settings of those in training. Supervisors and managers of staff can be encouraged through training to recognise and respond to personal and professional dilemmas of work in this area. They will need also to be alerted to policy issues which may arise from this area of work, particularly in relation to residential establishments. For residential workers in training, it will be important to allow an opportunity to address policy issues and guidelines of residential establishments for dealing with the issues raised.

Issues around the gender and sexual orientation of trainers will arise with a new focus when training in working with boys. The race, gender and sexual orientation of those selected for work in this field will also need consideration as it does in all work with sexual abuse. There is a variety of opinion on professionals working with victims of the opposite and same sex. Sexual orientation is another aspect of this broader question. Trainers and managers need to consider this dimension and develop training which includes recognition of the possible differences in perspective arising from heterosexual and homosexual experience, and which prepares workers to incorporate their own perspective in a sound professional approach.

Theoretical perspectives

The preceding papers are written by workers who operate from a range of theoretical perspectives and who take different views on some of the issues in working with boys. This can be reflected in the training context where different options for work can be described but it will be important that the theoretical basis is clearly stated.

Summary

Many of the issues in training for work with boys will have been covered in good basic training for work with sexually abused children generally. There is, however, increasing evidence that the incidence, patterns and consequences of sexual abuse of boys differ from that of girls. It is essential that the development of knowledge in this area can be maintained by trainers in order to ensure that general and specific training can be sensitive and alert to the differences at every stage of work with abused children.